THE COMPLETE BOOK OF MOUNTAIN SPORTS

Don't be a spectator! Join the *doers!* Hiking, climbing, backpacking . . . downhill skiing, cross-country skiing, snowshoeing, snowmobiling. It's all here in the world of mountain sports. Learn about what gear you'll need, what kind of clothes, where to go, techniques, safety rules. Get in touch with nature, but respect the mountains and environment. Use caution and good sense in your sport. Your rewards will be great ones as you become a participant in mountain sports.

THE COMPLETE BOOK OF Mountain Sports

Curtis W. Casewit

PHOTOGRAPHS

JULIAN MESSNER
New York

Published by Julian Messner, a Simon & Schuster
Division of Gulf & Western Corporation, Simon &
Schuster Building, 1230 Avenue of the Americas,
New York, N.Y. 10020.

Manufactured in the United States of America

Design by Irving Perkins

Library of Congress Cataloging in Publication Data

Casewit, Curtis W
The complete book of mountain sports.

Bibliography: p. 185
Includes index.
SUMMARY: Discusses the necessary clothing and equipment, techniques, safety rules, and places to go for a variety of mountain sports including hiking, climbing, backpacking, downhill skiing, cross-country skiing, and others.
1. Outdoor recreation–United States–Juvenile literature. 2. Mountains–Recreational use–Juvenile literature. [1. Outdoor recreation. 2. Mountains–Recreational use] I. Title.
GV191.4.C37 796.5′0973 78–15901
ISBN 0–671–32902–2

Acknowledgments

I would like to thank many people for their help with this book. They were generous with interviews or wrote me at length. They read chapters or helped me test their products. They furnished the photos and dug up much helpful data. Among many others, I'd like to express my thanks to Bill Forrest, crack climber and president of Forrest Mountaineering Equipment; Georg Kroll, Kneissl Skis of America; J. F. Lanvers, binding expert at Look Sports; John Malo, who knows a lot about Midwestern elevations; Herb Saltford, the New York "birder"; Mike Frome, one of the leading authorities on National Parks and National Forests; Win Willis, Colorado Mountain Club; Ed Hunter of the Winter Park Ski Resort; Lois Barr, Keystone, Colo.; Rick Marsh and Bill Evans, Rocky Mountain Ski Tours, Rocky Mountain National Park; Art Lang, High Country Inn Summer Camp; and Policano, Inc. which introduced me to "Presun," which saved my skin at long stints in high altitudes. Lastly, I'm grateful to Jon Wood for additional research and to my teenage son Niccolo, elite climber, super ski racer, good XC-man, for much information.

Contents

CHAPTER 1

Mountain Joys

WHAT YOU FIND UP THERE

As you cross the brow of a hillside, the mountain suddenly appears before you.

You first saw it from the valley. But the peak looks bigger now, more massive. You see the band of forest at the base, and higher up, there are large rock walls. The thin line of a foot trail leads up a ridge. A patch of eternal snow gleams on the summit.

You're drawn to the mountain. You're on vacation here with your parents, and as you stop to survey the scene, your senses are sharper than usual. You listen to the sound of the wind coming up from the meadows. You catch the sweet scent of the young fir trees. The color of the sky seems bluer than at home.

You'll be hiking for a few hours. Or you could be backpacking and spending a night in these mountains.

If you happen to stay at a resort in rocky country, you could also be part of a rock-climbing party. Some mountain towns offer teaching programs.

The same setting serves you in winter when you ski here. Or snowshoe. Or reach certain areas in a caravan of snowmobiles.

You've entered the vast world of mountain sports.

I have personally tried all of these, skiing and hiking for nearly four decades. To write about it, I took several rock-climbing courses and traveled to a glacier in the Pacific Northwest for instruction in ice scaling. My teenage son, after many years of experience, races on a ski team and leads younger people up steep rock walls. My daughter tried these and other mountain sports, too, making friends en route and learning much about the environment as well.

THE JOYS OF HIKING

Remember that you don't need 14,000-foot-high peaks for your outdoor activities. You can chalk up some good hiking mileage on a weekend in Texas' Chisos Mountains at Big Bend National Park. The relatively low (1,500–2,500 ft.) Ozarks offer plenty to the young backpacker. Pikes Peak, Mt. Hood, and Mt. Washington can all wait.

For now, enrich your summer in the nearest hills. After many years of hiking, we have learned that there can be a reward at the end of the trail. This includes the unexpected moments when you discover a cave or come upon a deserted gold mine. Your destination may be a 1,000-foot mountain top where you can see the route you've come. On the summit, you appreciate the altitude you gained and perhaps put your name into the summit register. How about a fire lookout? There is not only a view, but also perhaps a forest ranger, who tells you how his instruments work or what he hears on the radio.

One summer, while in the Sawtooth Mountains of Idaho, we saw a small lake on a map. We set out for it. The lake was as blue as a baby's eye, and we got the impression that almost no one had been there before. My twelve-year-old son caught rainbow trout with his bare hands, and we vowed we'd come back.

Mountain joys begin with a hike into a meadow where you can admire the flowers. *(Peter Runyon Photo, Vail, CO)*

Your hiking goal can be a spring, an ancient logging camp, or just a forest full of wild strawberries.

GETTING IN TOUCH WITH NATURE

You must move slowly to get in touch with nature. There are young hikers who catch and seriously collect butterflies. The young wilderness photographer positions himself on a plateau, content to sit still, all patience, waiting for the herd of deer or other creatures. Over the crest, down the backside of the same mesa, a young woman begins to move uphill to examine a wildflower that goes by the name of Indian paintbrush. The hiking amateur botanist must go and study the vegetation on the summit. He walks and pauses, bending down to inspect a round green pin cushion; he notices that the mosses come in many colors and shapes. Each of the species has its own tiny flowers and leaves.

If you should ever hike up to higher elevations–a 4,000-footer in New England or a peak in the Rockies–you can't help admiring the hardiness of the flora. How is it possible that the plants do not die in winter? What makes tiny wildflowers get along with less oxygen and more radiation? How do some mountain flowers manage to spite the short summers and harsh climate above timberline? Keep in mind that smallness helps. The tinier the leaves, the less resistance to the wind. A sense of amazement must fill you at some mountaintop discoveries. You'll learn about some of these wonders in the chapter on backpacking.

The mountain hiker may also begin to understand the world of birds. After all, on foot you have enough time to study a tree; it may be occupied by the nests of several bird species. Like a family of mountain chickadees, a childless mountain bluebird, or a woodpecker, who builds a home for himself as well as for others. In your mountain travels, you may see Alpine crows, black ravens, hummingbirds, larks, thrushes, and waterfowl such as mallard ducks, Canadian geese, and snow geese, all at various elevations.

CLIMBING

You'll hear more about these hiking fringe benefits in the next chapter. You'll also find out how to pace yourself on the trail.

Joys of the winter outdoors. *(John Wilson)*

Young people, just like their elders, welcome the privacy found in the mountains.

You can escape from the crowds; all you need are your legs and good lungs. A national park may bustle with cars and shuttle buses. But walk a mere five miles, and you've left most of humanity behind you. As a hiker you will find peace by venturing just a few thousand feet above the overflowing resort towns, or by striking out on foot beyond the hillside of your hometown.

It's a relatively short step from hiking to climbing.

The hike up a steep trail can be considered a "climb" and so will the scramble up a series of rocks that resemble stairs. Such climbing requires no ropes or other gear. The closest river may have some stone slopes which you can handle that way.

The height of a mountain is not very important. The boulders and cliffs that are strewn all over the United States like so many rugged marbles can serve your first efforts. You'll discover small rock upthrusts and rocky ridges even in the whcatlands of the Midwest. Yosemite and Yellowstone are breathtaking, but you will also enjoy the Black Hills of South Dakota and the jagged cliffs of the Hudson Valley in New York.

You can climb impressive 100-meter towers in Arizona or explore the ledges and ocean-lapped stone formations of the Pacific Coast. Rock climbing lends itself to learning more about geology.

Long-time mountain guides will assure you that most young people show a knack for rock scrambling. They're naturals. They're sure-footed. They have good balance and coordination.

Experts always warn you, though, that it would be unwise to climb alone. Or to string along with another flatlander who has never scaled a rock face.

You'll learn about the basic climbing techniques and equipment in Chapter 4; it should be said here, though, that there are all kinds of climbing levels. As you get better, you will attack rock only with companions of equal skill. You'll use ropes and some hardware for safety. In time, you'll meet "rock engineers" who can scale a rock face only with great amounts of specialized gear; other young people–the "free" climbers –bring the bare minimum of equipment. These young people are already so skilled that they can handle difficulties with just a nylon rope for safety.

Whatever their methods, young men and women climb in search of freedom, adventure, and, in some cases, thrills.

Many cragsmen welcome the dizzying heights, the varied dangers, and the battle with oneself. These young people work hard to overcome their fears, to strengthen their self-control. They attempt to keep their cool in the middle of a slick wall.

A few daredevils seek only the most hairy climbs or the greatest heights, vertical excursions up the very seams of the earth.

We'll give you details about some of their ambitions and achievements and how they talk to one another. Most of these climbers have their own language. Many of the finest ones are often under eighteen years of age.

To be sure, advanced mountaineering strips character down to the bones. A few minutes on a rock spire with a fellow can tell a girl more about him than five weeks in school. On a ledge, no one can fake anything. Words hardly count here; only mature action. Everyone's life is at stake. A sense of responsibility counts.

This kind of mountain sport is for only a few. Nor do many kids venture into the white, icy kingdom of the glacier. Climbing among 100-foot-deep glacier crevasses is a special world. It will be covered later.

DOWNHILL SKIING

Most young people stick to hiking in the summer. During winter, many teens head for the nearest lift-served area for some downhill skiing.

Many resorts now have lodges and apartments for sports families. *(Summit County)*

Never tried it? Catch a ride to a small ski area next weekend. There will be a base lodge with a sundeck, from which you can usually watch a ski slope. A lot of high schoolers are up there. Study them.

You notice how a young girl is cutting a swath through the bright white hillside. She may not be very experienced, but you can see her blond pigtails bobbing. As she zooms by you, she lets out a wild yodel. She isn't showing off; she is just having the time of her life. Some people can't help singing or hollering with joy, or taking leaps.

There are other kinds of young skiers. Some of them frequently stop and look back at the hill. They like the silence of the scene. Perhaps it gives them fresh strength for school the next day. In the meantime, each day trip is like a little vacation.

Why take up skiing? If you're a skier now, you already know the freedom of darting, leaping, and weaving downward through a white world. You know that skiing can be a lark, exploration, total flight, a moment of truth, a battle with the elements, total quiet, a ballet dance, a sunbath, and always a health giver. Small children do it; teenagers excel at it after a few lessons.

Skiing instruction is now streamlined around North America. The schools generally favor two half-day lessons and then get you up the lifts and onto trails. You begin by learning how to "herringbone" up a hill, to glide down a gentle incline without a fall. The next step is the "wedge," which becomes your brake, and your start toward the first turns. Climbing and traversing on skis will become easy; and the all-round activity feels good. As a novice you'll work up a lather in fifteen minutes.

Finally, there is the first straight downhill run–the *schuss,* as your instructor calls it–and the first, wonderful curve. It is a triumph. Before long you've become an intermediate skier. You can now venture further and go faster.

To the advanced skier, speed is a joy. There is also the challenge of freshly fallen snow. The expert loves skiing the white, virgin powder snows. Your leg muscles have become strong; they absorb the ever-changing terrain.

Finally, for a few, there is always another possibility. They'll go in for ski racing. Various races for both boys and girls will be briefly discussed. Should you enter a slalom meet? Or try the downhill? Will you have the time to train for more serious junior competition? That's up to you, of course. The information in Chapter 8 should help you decide.

CROSS-COUNTRY SKIING

"Cross-country skiing," also known as "ski touring," simply means skiing without the benefit of mechanized lifts. That makes it much cheaper, of course. (The equipment is less expensive, too.) Naturally, cross-country skiing (also known as "XC") isn't for speed freaks. You go slowly. Your legs do all the work to move you uphill, and because of the narrow skis, the downhills are comparatively tame.

The slow pace usually makes the XC skier appreciate the wilderness more than the lift-skier. The XC enthusiast (and the even slower snowshoer) sees not only the sharpened outlines of faraway ranges, but also the sun-dipped treetops and the tracks of snowshoe rabbits.

Cross-country makes use of the trail networks at the larger resorts that build many miles of paths to please the ski tourers. Or you can head for special trails in national forests, state forests, and national parks. XC will lead to parts of a mountain that are new to you. This turns you into an explorer. You're a Meriwether Lewis or William Clark or Robert Peary. Any new trail—whether it's in New Jersey or in Minnesota—has a mystery about it. But when you go touring in the higher mountains, such as the Rockies, the sensation of a new discovery is even more overpowering. The explorer on XC skis never knows what is around the next corner.

Cross-country skiing, snowshoeing, and some other mountain sports bring you in contact with the elements. The shoulders of the nearest mountains may be swimming in the purest sunlight. Or you can pick a cold day. The brooding clouds will open and the thick flakes muffle all sounds. You pull out the hood and fasten the yellow goggles. You're likely to turn back. But you return home that night with a sense of the primitive.

Somehow, the young XC skier or snowshoer is in tune with long-gone days when there were neither automobiles nor motor bikes. The jet hadn't been invented yet. There were few trains.

Even on a protected two-mile XC trail, the modern skier can be reminded of the American West in the 1850s, of hardy, blizzard-battling people like Snowshoe Thompson. (He was a

Mountain joys are shown in this picnic shot. *(Aspen Ski Corp.)*

skiing mail carrier in the Sierras, on whose strength depended entire mining camps. He would be on his long slats for days, carrying a heavy pack across the deep snows, where horses had floundered.)

Cross-country skiing still gives the chance to match wits with a mountain. It doesn't have to be very famous or very far away. It can even be an icy hill in New York State. But every inch of the run presents a new challenge.

Snowshoeing can be done wherever you find deep snow. It takes only a minimum of time. No long drives are necessary; no full days are required. These winter hikes on webbed supports can be done in a few hours. A short winter afternoon will do fine. You need not go to a posh winter sports mecca for this healthy recreation; the local midwestern or Canadian foothills can be just as satisfactory.

You'll soon read more about the gear and tactics of both XC and snowshoeing. (We have even included a page on how to make your own shoes.) And there will be an introduction to some mountain sports that may be new to you.

THE PLEASURES OF SNOWMOBILING

Lastly, you may want to know about snowmobiling. The people of Wisconsin, Minnesota, Michigan, and Ontario are very familiar with it.

You can conquer many a hill on a snowmobile. The machine does your bidding. Turn the handle bar, and you have great power. The machine surges forward and up a hillside.

Teenagers can learn how to steer snowmobiles. Certain areas of the country have been designated for them. In Chapter 10 you'll learn where the trails are and how not to destroy the environment. (Many people have mixed feelings about this mountain sport, and we'll examine their views.)

As you can see, this book isn't for spectators. It's for *doers.*

How much can you do without your parents? Quite a lot. How often can you get into some of these mountain sports? As often as you can reach the nearest hillside.

Respect the moods of a mountain. Use some caution. Your rewards will be rich ones.

CHAPTER 2

Hiking

WHY ANYONE CAN HIKE

One of my son's favorite hikes begins on a 300-foot mountain 10 miles from our home. The trail can be reached by bus. On weekday afternoons, there are few people on this gentle footpath. It goes on for about 6 miles. How far do you want to go? You can decide that on your own. You see nature, not houses. You smell wild grasses, not gas fumes. You hear no squeals of car tires. Instead, the birds twitter. Squirrels may race across your path.

The vegetation up there changes all the time. First you're in the open, with a few grassy slopes below you. Next there are leaf trees. Then you walk under conifers. Sometimes the path skirts large boulders covered with mosses or lichen.

Anyone who can walk can hike there. Even the smallest child. You see families with children under ten. On occasion, you meet Boy Scout groups. On Sunday afternoons, you spot young couples and middle-aged people.

The "Beaver Brook Trail" is typical of many around North America. There are thousands like it, and probably some right near your home.

Anyone can walk for an hour or two. Hiking for a few hours in gentle terrain doesn't take great strength.

A few miles of hill-walking doesn't even require much endurance. You move naturally, easily, across the sloping face of the land.

Hiking doesn't cost anything. You don't need money to do it. You clearly see so much more on the foot trail than in a car. And you feel better about the experience. You *earned* the top of a mountain! An Illinois teacher puts it this way: "If you ride to a summit in an automobile, you say, 'Man, isn't it pretty?' and forget it. But when you hike up, you remember every terrain feature, every twig, every turn in the trail. It'll be a great memory for the rest of your life."

DISTANCES AND PACING

How far can young people ages ten to thirteen walk? That depends on physical condition. Do you do a lot of other sports? Or do you spend most of the time watching television? Even so, six mountain miles is not too much for a healthy young person. Some youngsters have no trouble doing a 12-mile round trip across hilly country. Their second outing can be increased to 15 miles. After some short trips, a full morning or all day hike isn't too much.

How about elevation gain? Up to 500 feet is easy. Conditioned young hikers can climb 2,500 feet per day without strain. Naturally, the steeper the ascent, the more effort is required.

Want a more scientific explanation? One mountain club divides the different hikes into the following groups:

Class A: Easy trips with a maximum distance of 8 miles round trip and an altitude gain of up to 1,000 feet.

Class B: Trips involving a maximum distance of up to 12 miles round trip with an altitude gain of 1,000 to 2,500 feet.

Class C: Hikes of up to 15 miles round trip with an altitude gain of up to 4,000 feet. Rock-scrambling, steep grass, or other rough terrain problems are involved, but no knowledge of rock climbing is required for these outings.

Distances? You'll increase them with experience. You may have read about various high school classes being challenged by (and doing) a fifty-mile hike in hilly regions.

One western teenager likes to knock off *several* high peaks on a Sunday. "Might as well do two instead of one," he says. His record is 8,000 vertical feet in a single day.

How fast should you go? Take it easy, especially the first time. Forget about your city pace, where you race all the time. Go slow.

You see more the leisurely way. "I think a hiker is entitled to watch a chipmunk," says an Idaho guide. "Or to pause once in a while and scan the landscape for elk and mountain goats. That's one purpose of a mountain travel."

The too rapid tempo exhausts you much more quickly. Even a good junior athlete may peter out if he *runs* the first uphill mile at top speed. That's why most experts believe in the wise advice that, "who goes into the mountains fast, comes out last!" Or, as an old English proverb says it: "Too swift arrives as tardy as too slow. . . ."

HOW NOT TO GET TIRED

Most experienced leaders peg their pace to the slowest, youngest person of the group. A slow, flowing upward motion works out best, with a brief (standing) rest every half hour. Mountain guides believe in "pausing" rather than "stopping." You never sit down except for meals.

Always remember that your upward trek is limited by heartbeat and lung power. It's also wisest to avoid competition on a mountain hike. Not long ago, for instance, a sixteen-year-old drove his father so hard and recklessly on a New England climb that the aging parent collapsed with a heart attack. The 4,000-foot elevation of the trail had much to do with it. Sure, you won't have to cope with altitudes in the Midwest. But if you come from sea level to the New England ranges, you may feel somewhat breathless or dizzy at first. Give in. Likewise, certain western states like Colorado, Utah, Wyoming, and Montana have high ranges that affect the hiker, especially if you have just arrived from the flatland or the coast.

Bear in mind that you'll get less tired in the Rockies by *walking* less on your first day. Particularly if you have just arrived from Chicago, Omaha, or Kansas City.

At 9,000 feet, the air is markedly thinner. The oxygen content is still about 21 percent, but now you are taking in less air with each breath. At 11,000 feet–common in the Rockies–or 14,000 feet, the diminution of oxygen does some subtle things to your mind and body. You may feel short of breath and somewhat sluggish. You may even develop a slight headache. These are all common and temporary symptoms of your body adjusting to the altitude change. They all should pass. (It takes about one day per 1,000 feet.)

Naturally, even getting tired has its advantages. You'll sleep better and feel more refreshed the next day.

SOME INEXPENSIVE HIKING ESSENTIALS

Walking on uneven surfaces happens to benefit your feet. But for the best footwork, you need to be protected by sturdy, comfortable hiking boots–the first essential. Avoid leather soles; pick a sole with rubber or Vibram lugs.

Where should you buy the boots? Not necessarily in one of those mountaineering or specialty stores. Most regular shoe shops stock hiking boots at less cost to you or your parents. You can usually get bargains at department stores like Sears Roebuck, Penney's, or Montgomery Ward. Fortunately, such footwear can also be worn to school or for winter travel. Wise hikers break in their new boots before trying them on a long hiking expedition.

Buy boots that are large enough for two pairs of socks. (Good heavy wool socks and a thinner pair are the best combination for most purposes.) Tennis shoes are okay for a short stroll through the woods or on good trails in the flat country. But tennis shoes won't give adequate padding or support, particularly on a mountain trail.

Sneakers won't do you much good in wet or rocky regions. Avoid tennis shoes on ice. In one instance, a boy tried to tackle an Oregon glacier in tennis shoes. He started sliding and crashed against the rocks, fracturing one arm. As for street shoes, they are *never* worn on mountain hikes.

Loafers, gym shoes, or moccasins make a welcome change in the evening after heavy boots on the trail.

Loose-fitting pants and shirt insure you against chafing and rubbing. A hat, sweater, lightweight parka, or waterproof poncho give you comfort in case of rain or snow. Remember, winterlike conditions can be encountered at higher elevations even in the summer. You can always shed clothes to cool off, but you can't put them on if they're back home.

A small, individual pack or knapsack is a necessity for a day hike. After all, you don't want to carry your extra clothes or your lunch in your hands. Besides, a full day pack will prepare you for backpacking later that year or the next season. A ninety-pound junior hiker can easily carry ten to fifteen pounds on his or her back. You may take along a few candy bars, prepackaged sandwiches, a thermos with fruit juice, an extra pair of socks, a sweater, gloves, sun cream, and most important, a waterproof parka. Someone in your group may bring a camera, binoculars, a small first-aid kit, a whistle, a compass, map, matches, knife, pencil, and notebook.

GETTING THE MOST PLEASURE FROM YOUR TRIP

You can go on hikes for any number of reasons. It's good to know your own mind; you'll get more out of the trip that way. For instance, you may go along because your father and mother invited you; normally you don't see them much, and you realize that a joint mountain venture will bring your family closer together. (In fact, some teens suggest such outings to their folks.)

Other young people take up this mountain sport for the sake of exercise; they're aware of the benefits. One of these is that frequent hiking strengthens your muscles and removes poundage from those who are overweight. You may walk for two hours in the company of friends because you know of a certain lake where the fishing is excellent. Collecting gems, studying rocks, and examining fossils all fetch some hikers. Making a certain summit—"Hey! Our class climbed to the top of Pike's Peak!"—is yet another reason. Weather stations or scientific installations (where scientists study cosmic rays, for example) make interesting destinations.

The listing of the various hikes at one national park gives you a clue to still more possibilities.

Tuesday

7:00 A.M. Bird Walk. Meet at Park Visitor Center.
8:30 A.M. Half-day hike to waterfalls. Meet at Wild Basin ranger station.
8:30 A.M. Half-day hike to Lake Haiyaha. Meet at Bear Lake parking area.
10:00 A.M. Two-hour walk to study the geology of the area.
10:00 A.M. Tundra Nature Walk.
11:30 A.M. One-hour walk in Sprague Lake area, followed by picnic.
7:30 P.M. Beaver walk. Limit thirty people. Observe beavers at work.

There is a camp near Steamboat Springs, Colorado, where some of the day excursions deal mostly with botany. Thanks to a botanist in charge of the camp, the eleven to fourteen year olds pick mushrooms (Which ones can you eat? Which ones are poisonous?) and look for edible plants. They also study the wildflowers at various periods and elevations.

What a variety! Naturalists estimate that there are some 6,000 species in the Rockies. Who can doubt it? Just go to the foothills and then higher up, repeating your hikes each month.

Hikers often see scenes like this one. *(Swiss National Tourist Office)*

As the snow disappears from one particular Colorado area, the mountains bring forth a rush of Easter daisies, marigolds, wild sweet peas, fairy trumpets, pink rock hill phlox, and other flowers in many colors.

In early summer the campers wander up to Colorado's 8,000- or 9,000-foot levels. Here, almost overnight, they see leafy cinquefoils, arnicas, yellow monkey flowers, and the official state flower, the Colorado columbine.

In July the hikers will be welcomed by the star gentians, wood lilies, the mountain asters, and several kinds of larkspur. Above 10,000 feet the young botanists walk among crimson Indian paintbrushes, blue violets, chiming bells, harebells, Alp lilies, and shooting stars in the flashiest colors. Above 12,000 feet in these Rockies, you see alpine forget-me-nots and mountain phlox, all with long roots and tiny bodies. Naturally, the higher one climbs, the later the season for wildflowers. In the span of a summer, though, many of the youngsters remember most of the names of the plants they saw.

Such knowledge will last a lifetime.

WHO TO GO WITH

What if your parents are too busy to take you hiking? Or if your school doesn't have a program? Consider a summer camp, a mountain guide, a hiking club. Or think about hikes guided by ranger-naturalists, men who describe the trees, plants, animals, and geology of a national park.

There are all kinds of possibilities for finding company for hikes. The suggested list that follows has some familiar names, the Boy Scouts of America, for instance. But you'll need the addresses so that you can find out the nearest chapter. Certain national groups may also be overlooked by young people or teachers. Yet many of these larger organizations include hiking in their programs.

Here are some good contacts for you. Take the initiative and write a few letters asking for information.

Useful Addresses

American Youth Hostels, 6300 Fifth Avenue, Pittsburgh, PA 15232 (Many different coast-to-coast programs.)

Adirondack Mountain Club, Glen Falls, NY 12801 (A large, well-established organization.)

The American Forestry Association, 1319 18th Street, N.W.

Washington, DC 20036 (Offers much information on conservation.)

Appalachian Mountain Club, 5 Joy Street, Boston, MA 02108 (The Club runs many outings and excursions for the day, weekend, week or for more extended periods. Chapters of the A.M.C. exist in New York, Connecticut, Rhode Island, Springfield, MA, Worcester, MA, New Hampshire, Portland, OR, and the greater Philadelphia area.)

The Appalachian Trail Conference, Inc., 1718 N Street, N.W. Washington, DC 20036 (One of the oldest, best-known groups.)

Boy Scouts of America, New Brunswick, NJ 08903 (Write there to find out about programs near your home.)

Camp Fire Girls, 1740 Broadway, New York, NY 10019 (May have hiking groups in your vicinity.)

The Colorado Mountain Club, 2530 W. Alameda Avenue, Denver, CO 80219 (Offers many year-round hikes for young people.)

Canadian Mountain Holidays Ltd., 130 Banff Avenue, P.O. Box 1660, Banff, Alberta, Canada (Ask them about their "Young Explorer" groups.)

The Canadian Youth Hostel Association, 270 Maclaren Street, Ottawa or Sherbrooke W., Montreal, Quebec, Canada (Maps and programs.)

Girl Scouts of the USA, 830 Third Avenue, New York, NY 10022. (Inquire about group nearest your home.)

Green Mountain Club, P.O. Box 94, Rutland, VT 05701 (An old, established group.)

High Country Inn, P.O. Box 96, Winter Park, CO 80482 (Nice summer hiking programs for youngsters.)

The Mountaineers, Box 122, Seattle, WA 98111 (Junior groups for ages fourteen and up go on hikes.)

Nahsta Outdoor School at Vail, P.O. Box 7421, Colorado Springs, CO 80907 (Summer programs for ages twelve and up.)

The New York-New Jersey Trail Conference, P.O. Box 2250, New York, NY 10001 (Has list of many hiking clubs.)

Northern Lights Alpine Recreation, P.O. Box 299, Invermere, British Columbia, Canada (Some hiking treks and camps.)

Omaha Walking Club, 5301 Jackson, Omaha, NB 68101 (Hiking in the Midwest.)

The Sierra Club, 530 Bush Street, San Francisco, CA 94108 (Family knapsack tours all over the country, with camps scattered from the Olympic Mountains in Washington State to the Adirondacks in northern New York State.)

The Wilderness Society, 4260 E. Evans Avenue, Denver, CO 80222 (Sponsors some hiking trips.)

SOME HIKING TIPS FOR JUNIOR LEADERS

If you don't have access to these organizations in your area, you may want to form your own group of friends or schoolmates for occasional outings. Hopefully, you've already chalked up some experience in the outdoors. Experienced hikers who have tried the flatlands generally realize that mountains require additional hiking knowledge, even low mountains.

For instance, you'll no doubt discourage friends who want to go *alone* into a wilderness region. You're aware that one hikes in company for the sake of safety. You know from previous trips that the leader tells *someone* where the group is going. You could inform a Forester or Park Ranger, the local sheriff, a sports shop, some friends, or your parents. When you return from the hike, make it a point to check back with them. (If you *don't,* a rescue party may be sent after you!)

Because you're in charge, it will be your responsibility to

protect the environment at all times. You'll prevent your hiking party from throwing away candy wrappers, leaving empty cans of pop, or strewing any other garbage along the trail. (Some clubs actually organize "clean-up hikes," where people collect the junk tossed away by others.)

You'll see to it that your members don't pick the flowers. In that respect, some hiking clubs have good sayings like:

> "Take only memories. Leave only footsteps. . . ."
> "Take nothing but pictures, leave nothing but tracks!"

Most leaders obey the rules of *courtesy* when it comes to private farmlands. For instance, they'll make sure to close all the gates behind them, so that cattle can't escape. They never take dogs along, and good leaders stick to existing trails, knowing that mountain slopes and forest lands are perishable. Off-trail footsteps eventually cause erosion. That's why most young conservationists take such a dim view of trail (motor) bikes, jeeps, and other vehicles.

HIKING SAFETY

It's also true that off-trail travel could get you lost. An entire chapter will deal with certain mountain sports dangers. But a few pointers may come in handy here.

Just as the leader sets the right pace, so the leader decides on the route at all times. No one can argue with the experienced boy or girl in charge. (There is nothing wrong with telling the leader that you're afraid of some terrain, though. Feel free to ask for help when you come to a difficult place on a trail. Accept an outstretched hand!)

At times, the person in charge will suggest that someone is not strong enough to complete an extremely long hike. The leader will perhaps ask that you go back to a safe place with another person. Or the group may decide to go on and complete the hike. You may be told to wait until the group returns. On longer hikes, particularly for large numbers of people, the leader will appoint a "rear guard." This rear leader makes sure that even the slower individuals–the stragglers –are safe. No one should be left behind.

On some occasions, the entire group will have to turn back before reaching the day's objective. This takes some pleasure out of your trip, but it could save your life. You must anticipate the strength of your party for the return trip. Weather could add to the difficulty. Fog obscures your landmarks. Rain makes descent treacherous. Wind will steal your body heat. Thunder and lightning will demand a hasty retreat from all high points and ridges.

Mountain weather *is* capricious. The green forested state called Oregon can be sunny at one altitude and foggy a few feet higher up. The Rockies can blaze with sunshine at noon. Suddenly, out of nowhere, you see clouds. Then comes heavy rain, which transforms steep trails and fallen logs into wet chutes. You can be sent sprawling unless you go slowly.

Sometimes, too, the thunder rolls and the green pines turn

Masses of hikers in Colorado. *(Boulder Chamber of Commerce)*

black. It's no dishonor to turn around when you notice the approach of nasty weather. Some of the most experienced hikers have given up before they've become soaked by a thunderstorm. But what if you're caught and lightning starts to flash overhead?

Get off a bare mountain and try to reach lower altitude. Never seek the shelter of an isolated tree. A large forest is less risky. You can also look for a cliff that is five or ten times your height. Spread out your knapsacks, rubberized rain jackets, or ponchos (folded several times). Let your group squat on these insulators.

WHERE TO HIKE

There are presently 104,600 miles of hiking trails in 154 national forests and 10,200 miles of trails in 32 national parks. Canada's provincial parks or the various provinces offer almost as vast a network for hikers.

Not all trails go through high mountains; our list will include walking mileage over gentle hills, too. Not every North American trail (not even all the *famous* ones) can be mentioned here. But a small sampling of ranges, regions, and possibilities in various states will get you started. (For more ideas, consult the books at the end of *The Complete Book of Mountain Sports.*)

U.S. East and Canada

In *New York* State, the *Tongue Mountain Range Trail* contains over 18 miles of foot trails. The most popular section of the system follows the ridge of Tongue Mountain 10 miles from its point on the lake to Route 9N, 12 miles north of Bolton Landing.

Finger Lakes Trail, New York (50 miles), links the Catskills and Allegheny Mountains across the base of the Finger Lakes to Niagara Falls. Contact the Finger Lakes Trail Conference, Inc., 22 Sturbridge Lane, Pittsford, NY 14534.

Still in New York State, the *Phoenicia Trail* to the Mt. Tremper Forest Fire Observatory starts at State Route 28 about a mile east of Phoenicia. The trail to the Belleayre Mountain Forest Fire Observatory from the Belleayre Mountain Ski Center, about 11 miles west of Phoenicia, is especially suited to the novice.

In *Virginia,* the *Mount Rogers Trail* is almost 5 miles long. You catch the trail at State Route 602, just east of Grindstone Campground, and go up to the north slopes of Mt. Rogers. The trail enters the edge of the spruce-fir forest. Wildflowers grow in abundance in late spring and summer.

In *New Hampshire,* the *New Hampshire Wilderness Trail* is a 9-mile-long trail starting at the junction about 4.7 miles from Lincoln. At 2.7 miles after you start, a side trail leads to the Franconia Brook Shelter; from there, another path leads to the spectacular Franconia Falls. The trail ends in *Maine* at Mt. Katahdin, a high point of 5,267 feet. (Hikers approach the granite peak from Millinocket.) Katahdin is a terminal point of the famous 2,000-mile-long *Appalachian Trail.* The latter begins in Georgia and traverses the Smokies, the hills of North Carolina, Virginia, and Maryland and then leads through the Blue Mountains of Pennsylvania, the Berkshire Hills of Massachusetts, New York's Adirondacks, and New Hampshire's White Mountains en route to Maine. The Trail also cuts through the length of Vermont's Green Mountains.

In *Canada* the 120-mile-long *Laurentide Trail* links 70 miles of trails in the hills of Ottawa's popular Gatineau Park with the rolling Laurentian Mountains, north of Montreal. The Laurentide passes near many Quebec villages with easy access to the trail for short hikes.

Midwest and South

In *Michigan,* try the *Ishpeming Trail* to Ishpeming Point. The climbing begins beyond the river. You pass maples, oaks, and white pine. About three-quarters of a mile from the top of Ishpeming Point, you cross a stream on a foot bridge. Beyond this, it really gets steep. At 1,377 feet, Ishpeming Point is high enough.

In the same state, the *Cross Michigan Hiking Trail* (210 miles) winds across the northern part of Michigan's Lower Peninsula from a point between Empire and Elberta on Lake Michigan to Tawas City on Lake Huron. The trail goes over dunes and through forests.

In *Wisconsin,* the *Scuppernong Trail* is located in Waukesha County, three-quarters of a mile northeast of Highway 67. The trail is located north of Eagle at the ranger station.

The 4-mile-long *Emma F. Carlin Trail* is located 1¼ miles east of Palmyra, Wisconsin, and south of Highway 59.

In *Oklahoma,* the 300-mile-long hilly *Trans-Ozark Trail* extends from the Oklahoma border across the northern part of the state to Salado through portions of the Ozark National Forest.

U.S. West, Northwest, and Southwest

In *California's* Yosemite National Park, the *Yosemite Falls Trail* is 7.2 miles round trip, unless you continue to Yosemite Point, which takes you over 8 miles. Expect many switchbacks. The starting point is Camp 4. Allow six hours. The view from the top is worth the effort.

For true wilderness hiking in the high country, try the famous *John Muir Trail.* It begins in Yosemite and goes south through Devil's Postpile to Sequoia/Kings Canyon and towering Mt. Whitney.

In *Wyoming* and *Idaho,* Yellowstone Park's *Waterfall Hike* can be reached from Ashton, Idaho, on Idaho State 47 (follow the Cave Falls signs).

The trail follows the west side of Falls River past Cave Falls and Bechler Falls. Go northeast, fording Boundary Creek and across the Bechler Meadows. The trail crosses the Bechler River. Less than one-half mile away to the north is Ouzel Falls with its 230-foot drop.

Wander up the canyon past Colonnade Falls. Have lunch

or a snack in the campground and then on to Iris Falls with its 45-foot drop. The hardy members of the party may continue up the canyon to the hot springs and Three River Junction. The Upper Bechler has at least six more waterfalls on the tributaries. The return is by the same route.

The *Sun Valley, Idaho Nature Trail* begins and ends at Trail Creek Cabin. Permanent trail markers are placed along the way for direction. Permanent stations list points of natural interest throughout the trail. Most flowers of short-blooming duration will be identified on a stake near their location.

Near Jackson, Wyoming, you'll find the *Swan Lake Nature Walk*. The three-hour loop hike goes to Swan Lake and Heron Pond. Elevations are from 6,800 feet to 6,900 feet.

The *Teton National Forest* outside Jackson, Wyoming, offers other hiking in unspoiled scenic backcountry famous for big-game herds.

New Mexico boasts the *Canadian River Trail* (130 miles) from Ute Lake to Springer, New Mexico, and the old Santa Fe Trail. This trail begins in Ute Lake State Park. The *Pecos River Trail* (100 miles) runs from Malaga south of Carlsbad, New Mexico, to Roswell along the Pecos River and through Bottomless Lake State Park.

Colorado is another big hiking state. In the Rocky Mountain National Park, for instance, the *Gem Lake* (8,800 feet) hike is a pleasant one for beginners. Drive north on Devil's Gulch Road from Estes Park. Trailhead, a marked horse trail, is less than a half-mile past MacGregor Ranch entrance, on the left. It runs 2½ miles one way at moderate steepness, though seemingly steeper just before the lake. In Boulder, Colorado, the beginner should try *Mt. Sanitas* (1,200 feet). It starts north of the road at the shelter house at the mouth of Sunshine Canyon, climbs bank and crosses a ditch, contours on south face of large rock outcropping, then reaches the ridge and follows it to summit. In Boulder, too, the *Flagstaff Mountain Trail* begins at the northwest corner of the turnoff to Baird Park from Flagstaff Road.

The scenic trail leads up the east slope of Flagstaff Mountain, with branches to Halfway House and a picnic site overlooking Boulder. It terminates on the summit.

In Colorado Springs, *Cheyenne Mountain,* elevation 9,563 feet, is worth a climb. The shortest route to the summit begins on Rock Creek. The South Cheyenne Creek saddle is about 6½ miles up old Stage Road from its start. Climb up the left side to the ridge crest and follow that northeast and then east of the summit.

Flattops Wilderness, Colorado, offers hiking. Drive east from Meeker (on Highway 40) to Trappers Lake campground, at the edge of the Flattops Wilderness area. Two good forest hikes here: One leads from the campground 6 miles to Fraser Lake on the border of the wilderness. The second is a 6-mile hike to Walls Lake, below Trappers Peak, within the wilderness area.

Arizona's Tonto Trail, Grand Canyon National Park (200 miles). This is considered the most challenging and dramatic by many hikers.

Washington State's *Miner's Lake Trail* is justly famous. Drive to Enumclaw and up to the top of Crystal Mountain. Walk down the service road to the trail that takes off to the right. The trail takes you across upper Lucky Shot ski slope and skirts five beautiful lakes (including Henskin) to Jim Town (an old mining camp). Then take Silver Creek trail to the valley floor. This puts you back to the beginning.

CHAPTER 3

The Total Backpacker and Camper

THE REWARDS OF BACKPACKING IN HILLY COUNTRY

Dawn in a deep forest 65 miles west of your community. Stars fading, sky turning lighter, then a blazing sunrise.

That early summer day, there were just two of us heading upward: an enthusiastic adult hiker and a preteen boy who loves the outdoors. City people both, in search of peace.

Backpacking fills people's needs. It sets you in motion, up wildflower-bordered paths, across small brooks and open meadows. You may see a waterfall or the full moon at night. This particular trip would consume only two days and two nights, bring us sights of eternal snow, of clear lakes filled with fish, and of sharp granite mountains. Moving up and down, we'd cross many geological zones, each with its own character, its own shapes, and colors. We'd cover about thirteen miles in all, carrying a hotel room on our backs. Challenging and unforgettable.

Backpackers go to the mountains for different reasons. But the rewards are always great.

For most young people, the trip becomes a key to the wilderness. You taste the solitude of nature. Naturalist John Muir, one of the earliest backpackers, wrote that "at night, in the depths of these woods, the stillness is sublime. . . ." When you sleep outdoors for the first time in your life—which you can do in dry, warm climates—you'll marvel at the stars overhead. You see them more clearly than you can in a city. You experience the world far more strongly outdoors, under the sky, than you do at home, in your own bed. If it rains, you hardly hear it under a city roof, but in a tent, you're very aware of a rainstorm. You sleep close to the earth and feel the pulse of the universe.

BACKPACKING AS A LEARNING EXPERIENCE

You can't fail to learn something on every trip, even on a short one. For instance, backpackers can pause to study a beaver pond. The beavers come out at night. They gnaw and saw trees, carrying away branches for their dams. If you put up your tent nearby, you'll see how these creatures swim, dive, run, dig canals, and fell trees. You can simply watch a wild rabbit, standing still for a few seconds until he leaps off and away. The antics of chickadees or of chipmunks can be funnier than the animals in television cartoons. One day while picnicking in a spruce forest, two gray birds—camp robbers—swooped down near, winging away with some crackers. The jays' daring action delighted everyone. On a lake, a few days later, a white trumpeter swan was seen. It is a fairly rare, graceful, proud bird, shy of humans.

The beauty of backpacking is that you can combine it with activities like bird watching, fossil viewing, or rock collecting.

A backpacker discovers that mountains come in all kinds of shapes. They can be lone pyramids like those in Alberta, Canada. They may be "domes" which you see in Yosemite National Park. Rock towers rise to hundreds of feet in New Mexico and Wyoming, where the "Devil's Tower" is typical. New England residents will be familiar with the polished peaks like Mt. Washington.

If you get into backpacking (and into some other mountain sports), your eyes will open to fresh geological knowledge. You can examine a deep canyon where the rock strata are exposed. The layers may change every few feet. The various formations often descend into a mountain for a mile or pile up high in one granite block. To the geologist there are not only the mountain's granite and other rocks, but there are also the rock-forming minerals like quartz, feldspars, and calcites. There are "metamorphic" rocks that changed because of temperature extremes and other reasons. A mountain can consist of igneous rocks, which were once part of volcanoes.

Young backpackers can also explore the 217-mile-long Grand Canyon in Arizona. Landslides, ice, frost, and water were at work here for millions of years. The Colorado River created canyon walls that soar straight up to 7,000-foot summits.

There are stunning 2,000-foot-high blocks and slabs with ledges and balconies under a blue sky. Backpacking geologists have found rocks in the Grand Canyon that go back many millions of years.

On a trip in the midwestern hill country, a teenager can become aware of the many life forms that appear and disappear with the seasons, adapting to climates, adding up to an ecological total. Take along a book so that you can identify wildflowers on the way uphill. In the summit meadows of higher mountains, known as "tundra," you will discover many miniature grasses, sedges, and herbs. If you brought a magnifying glass in your pack, you'd see details of almost microscopic leaves. You'll notice plants without any stems; others come with stems so short that the swirling air masses can't budge them. At the same time, the roots go down deep into the ground; a 2-foot root is the 2-inch plant's insurance against being ripped out by storms.

Amazing nature! The mountain sports devotee has a chance to appreciate all that nature has to offer. The person who never ventures away from home cannot experience these wonders.

BACKPACKING: A WAY TO INCREASE YOUR INDEPENDENCE

A young backpacker becomes more self-reliant, more independent than the stay-at-homes. After all, you provide for your own needs outdoors. You can't switch on the television for weather reports; you learn to read the sky. You cannot telephone your teacher for advice. As a backpacker you talk to your companions and make real friends.

Backpacking forces you to rely less on the comforts you're used to. In fact, there may be moments of unexpected discomfort. You may, for instance, become painfully tired at day's end. A shoulder may hurt, but you'll feel pride that you were able to carry twenty-five pounds for so many hours.

Surprises are always in store for young backpackers. Setting out alone recently, two teenage boys were caught by darkness among the sandstone cliffs in the foothills. The boys were sensible enough to set up camp at once. But they decided to spend the night on a bathtub-like rock. While they slept, clouds gathered overhead. They had brought no tent, and the rain began long before dawn. The water soaked their sleeping bags; it nearly washed the youngsters away. Wetness? A few shivers? A day of high fever? Small matter. "One loves life for having experienced it in very real and dramatic terms," wrote an early backpacker.

This is true, of course. Sometimes, we must feel rain water pouring down our cheeks. Or start a fire while it drizzles. We must occasionally itch with sweat. Or feel the needle prods of tired muscles. The backpacker faces the basics again. Hunger and thirst. The hot sun. The full use of limbs.

We may be on a footpath, yet we're off the beaten path. Away from billboards and interstate highways. Many campgrounds allow tents only–pickup campers, trailers, and motor homes are not permitted. The outdoor world of plains and mountains yields health and well-being.

BACKPACKING GEAR

Some young people are lucky enough to have cooperative parents who can afford to buy all their backpacking equipment. Other youngsters must do their own shopping from money they earned themselves or from allowances. Still other kids combine their folks' help with their own savings.

Fortunately, some of the hiking essentials can also be used for overnight trips. You can't backpack anywhere in tennis shoes, for instance, or in moccasins. You need the kind of hiking boots described in the previous chapter. The same goes for your clothes. These should keep you warm; even low mountains can get cold. And you need a waterproof slicker-type poncho or parka to keep you dry. The poncho must be large enough to fit over your pack.

How about the pack itself?

Remember that you can, at first, rent one. Many metropolitan cities now have special shops. Rentals are inexpensive. Take part in a free backpacking clinic held by some stores. It means an evening of slide shows, a lecture, and later a trial run. After a few short trips, you may want to buy your own things. Watch for sales at large sporting goods stores. Go to discount shops. Visit department stores. If you live in a large population center look into Sears Roebuck or Montgomery Ward; both sell some items at low prices. Specialty stores, while they can give you expert advice, always charge more.

There are all kinds of packs, depending on how many days you stay out and how often you go. For example, you can start with a small, cheap "day" pack if your parents intend to carry your heavy things. Some firms manufacture lighter equipment which allows you to haul about twenty pounds into the wilderness. For longer trips, a standard junior backpack will be needed. Begin with the least gimmicky one. Try out the pack and frame combination at the shop; the pack should ride well on your shoulders. The weight of modern backpacking products has been reduced, thanks to aluminum tubing

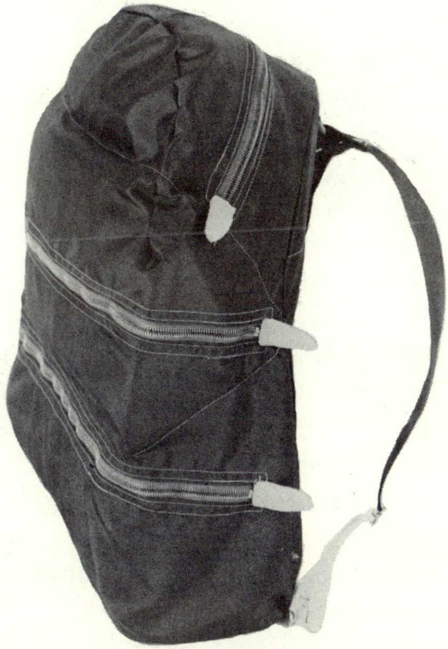

A light pack like this one is enough for a day's hike. *(Gerry Mountain Sports)*

and other features. Keep it simple. You don't require all sorts of zippered pockets or a leather bottom. Never mind fancy names or famous brands. A young person saves money by avoiding heavily advertised products. Some handy young people also consider the much less expensive "sew-yourself" packs, which can save a lot of money.

Once you own a backpack, you can use it for other purposes such as cross-country ski trips or bicycle outings.

Parents may buy the family tent or get a tent for you and a brother or sister. If you are going to get your own shelter, first ask yourself, "How often will I use a tent this summer? For just one night?" If this is the case, then a rental is still better. "Where will I camp?" In good climate, you can sleep without protection. A few dollars buys a "tube" tent that is open on both sides; this houses two young people. Umbrella-types will also sleep two young persons or adults.

A large sheet of plastic tied to a tree trunk or another type of "lean-to" may do the trick in warm regions. Sleeping under the stars can be pleasant if you bring an air mattress or a foam rubber pad. Both can be as comfortable as an innerspring mattress. Your leader will probably have camped in the area you're going to. Find out about nighttime temperatures. Inquire about the shelter situation. *In the high mountains* or in rainy regions you have no choice but to carry a tent.

Science has influenced equipment; there now exist extra-lightweight tents designed especially for the new backpacker. These outdoor products can take plenty of punishment. With a floor and a netting over the entrance, the shelters are insectproof, animalproof, and waterproof. The stakes are slightly larger than nails, and lightweight telescopic aluminum poles make for compactness.

The most expensive brands are not always the best. You may be better off with a simple army tent than the most advertised $250 job. Nor does the average young midwesterner require a "High Altitude" model (unless you head for high elevations) or an "Arctic Explorer" tent. Both of these models are built for high winds and snowstorms.

There are many ways to cut expenses. One of the backpacking ideas of the seventies? Outdoor gear kits for do-it-yourselfers. These kits allow you to sew your own tents and sleeping bags.

A sleeping bag is another necessity. You can rent one for that rare weekend of backpacking. You can also make a simple bag yourself from a single blanket by sewing it so that it is closed on three sides. The bags that you buy at an outdoor store, however, are generally made with nylon ripstop or taffeta cloth and filled with either goose down, duck down, or a synthetic material such as Dacron.

Goose down is generally considered the warmest, ounce for ounce. Duck feathers prove only 85 percent as effective as those of geese. Unfortunately, all down products are very expensive. For good reasons, too: down means feather-light sleeping bags. They roll up nicely and become less of a burden on your back. Garments filled with other materials are cheaper and not quite as warm; the synthetic fillings work out fine for summer trips into mountains lower than 2,500 feet. In fact, some Dacron bags test at below-zero temperatures. Most ranges in the South or Midwest never get that cold during summer nights.

What sort of shape should you choose? There are mummy-type bags and rectangular bags. The mummy type is tapered to fit your body, is the lightest to carry, and is the warmest. Some people find the mummy type too confining. By all means slip into the sleeping bag before you buy it; the store clerk should have no objections. As for sizes, think larger if you're still growing. Otherwise, you'll soon outgrow your bag.

Another tip: Don't let a salesman talk you into anything you don't need, or "trade you up" to a more expensive item than you want. Some young people get intimidated by the expert adult staff of specialty stores.

When it comes to your other articles like a parka, a windbreaker, a warm shirt, socks, a flashlight, and such, any general store will do. Specialty shops that cater to backpackers also charge more for food supplies. Buy them at a supermarket if possible.

Large grocery chains sell dried fruit, powdered orange juice, powdered cream, freeze-dried tea. Many backpackers also enjoy beef jerky, salami, smoked fish, nuts of all kinds, sunflower seeds, and chocolate. On longer outings consider taking lentils, rice, or spaghetti.

For just a couple of nights, plus two hiking days, you can pack items that give you plenty of food value, yet weigh little. Meat eaters? Bring steaks for the first dinner, perhaps precooked ham for the second. Wrap the meat in plastic and then foil. Place the packages inside your sleeping bag roll. Thanks to the insulation, your dinner won't thaw too soon.

If you're away from civilization for three to five days, you can now take advantage of modern inventions. Some backpackers' stomach satisfiers weigh just ounces. There are two types of concentrated foods—the freeze-dried and the dehydrated. Freeze-dried is the best because its flavors are almost like the real thing. These foods come in all kinds of varieties. You can get anything from scrambled eggs, soups, and vegetables to beef stew and chicken Italian-style. Even freeze-dried cheese cakes, pies, and, of course, ice cream. You'll find that freeze-dried items cost about twice as much as real ones. You are paying more because these products save you space and are lighter on your back.

The wilderness walker of the '70s is fortunate. Packs, tents, sleeping bags, and foodstuffs now rest easily on your shoulders. Your entire three-night baggage can amount to less than twenty pounds. (Some people prefer to take more equipment, which can amount to thirty or forty pounds.)

THE HOW OF BACKPACKING

Your backpack trip can be as easy or as hard as you want to make it. Hike fewer miles and go along a gentle, fairly level trail. Or make it super-sporty, and include a stint of steep climbing, with a heavier pack. On your first trip you should be accompanied by someone—parent, teacher, friend —who has done some backpacking before.

Just what physical fitness does this mountain sport take? Very little for short two-day trips on gentle slopes. Not much for the well-kept trails in hilly Massachusetts, for example, especially if you limit yourself to a few hours of walking before you set up camp. You don't have to be a superman (or superwoman) for midwestern outings. The 10,000 to 14,000-foot altitudes of the Colorado Rockies take more training and a few days of getting used to the thin air.

Don't try a week's backpacking in the western mountains if you haven't hiked before. You need some stamina for it. Unless you exercise you may not be in shape for long uphill trails.

There is truth in the philosophy of one club: "You just don't go backpacking, you *prepare* for it."

If you're a beginner, you can condition yourself to longer backpack expeditions by first going out for half a day. Carry a full pack. Get a feel for your equipment. Choose a route through easy terrain. See if the isolated country agrees with you. Expert guides claim that ten-year-olds can easily carry their own clothing and sleeping bags.

With enough training, anyone can take long weekend trips.

Experienced backpackers always suggest that you try out your equipment beforehand. Break in your new hiking boots. Stake out the new tent in your backyard. Make a freeze-dried dinner for yourself and some friends. (This allows you to test the new portable stove or to practice making a fire.)

Once you're on the trail, hiking won't be much of a hassle if you've worked up to it for some weeks. On the other hand, you may need some experience in where to set up camp.

Do it early in the afternoon; daylight makes it so much simpler. This way, you can also explore your camp neighborhood and avoid the difficulties of putting up your tent in the darkness.

A campsite should be chosen with some care. Avoid steep mountain slopes, where your tent and its occupants could roll down during the night. If you're in snow country, remember that snow "cornices" could break off. If it rains heavily while you sleep, a ravine could become a waterway; flooding could also occur if you camp too closely to a stream.

Select a level site without too many rocks. In fact, lie down on the ground. Stretch out before you put up the tent. Consider your needs. Is there a nearby water supply? Will you find some wood in the vicinity? Indeed, are you *allowed* to make wood fires?

It is always a good idea to ask about the local regulations ahead of time. For instance, whether you need a use permit to set up camp. You do need one in the national parks.

Advance reservations can be made for some parks. Otherwise, permits are available on a first come, first served basis.

You normally get permission to camp at specified areas in the remote backcountry. Permits will be limited to campsites accessible only by trail. Backpackers arriving after one area is closed usually have the chance of using another area in a national park.

If you're backpacking into a national forest, you'd be wise to call up the nearest U.S. Forest Service headquarters ahead of time.

Never drink from a pond or lake. Backpackers nowadays distrust streams and brooks as water supplies. The heavy use of wilderness areas makes it a good idea to purify your water.

Not all streams are contaminated. Since you never can tell, it is worthwhile to boil the water for at least twenty minutes. Chemical purification is also possible. Commercial preparations of chlorine and iodine-based chemicals are available.

Even if you're not the leader, it is important that you prepare for backpacking. Carry certain standard items for any overnight trip. Here's what the experts recommend:

Flashlight
First-aid kit
Pocket knife
Gum, candy, other snacks
Toilet tissue
Plastic whistle
Insect repellent
Small magnifying glass
Large-scale map of area
Compass
Waterproofed matches
Foil, 4 feet
Candle

The above is a minimum list. For longer or more complicated trips into high country, you need more items for survival, as well as emergency food and extra clothing.

WINTER CAMPING

Winter camping is a special pleasure because fewer young people do it. But this outdoor activity should not be recommended to beginners. Try some summer backpacking first. Chalk up some experience in bad weather. Then consider a one-night outing for the winter months.

Begin when temperatures are mild and avoid regions known for their blizzards or fierce colds. Backpackers find it easy enough to underestimate Mt. Washington (elevation 6,288 feet) in New England's Presidential Range. After all, doesn't a train go up? And a toll highway? However, winds can reach 100 mph speeds here. (The Mt. Washington Observatory once clocked record winds of 231 mph!) What's more, you may find the summit shrouded in a thick fog that cuts visibility to 30 feet. In winter, minus-40 degree temperatures are not unusual for Mt. Washington or the other Presidential Range peaks–Mt. Jefferson, Adams, Madison, Monroe.

Bear in mind that nature is much less forgiving in winter.

Father and son go backpacking. *(National Park Service)*

You must, therefore, prepare yourself to keep warm. A down sleeping bag becomes an essential, for instance. A down parka may be necessary. A shovel should be brought; it allows you to tunnel into a snow bank and build a snow cave. Start the job early in the day; make sure that your cave has ventilation and that the roof measures at least 1 foot of thickness.

The National Park Service considers the following minimum equipment for winter backcountry travel:

Stove–Gasoline-type best; for cooking, melting snow for water.
Extra food–high energy, no preparation.
Winter boots–multilayered boots are necessary.
Adequate clothing–windproof outer garments, wool pants and sweater(s), wool cap, mittens (not gloves), long underwear, gaitors (keep snow out of boots and legs dry), extra socks.
Repair kit and knife–tape, wire, cord, screws, etc.
Shelter–tent or snow cave shovel; lightweight groundcloth. The two will provide shelter.
Map and compass–practice use beforehand; "white out" blizzards are not uncommon.
Flashlight–gets very dark very early; extra batteries.
First-aid kit–help is a long way away in winter.
Dark glasses and goggles–winter sun and wind are intense; carry extras.
Face mask–a must item, high winds common above treeline.
Matches and candle–emergency fire starters.

The above list also applies to cross-country skiers and snowshoers.

ECOLOGY AND THE YOUNG BACKPACKER

For the past two decades, the Sierra Club has been sending groups of high school and college-age volunteers into wilderness areas, either to spend a week picking up cans or working alongside trail engineers building trails. The club sponsors many ecological work projects.

On a typical trip the young backpackers meet the leader and other trip members at a remote mountain roadhead. They will hike 5 or 10 miles to set up camp, and then start a plan of alternate work and free days. On off-days members hike, explore, read, or just sit around talking, swimming, and enjoying being away from it all. The work can be fairly rigorous sometimes, although anyone in good hiking condition can participate. The accent is on an easy mountain life, and everyone has a chance to share chores and cooking. Note that many of the cleanup and special projects offer a backpacking theme where you carry all you need into the backcountry.

Cleanup trips are jaunts into the hills to collect litter and debris left by less considerate campers. The wilderness is fragile. Trash that will not burn is sacked up so the rangers can pack it out. You may also help dismantle old hunter camps or remove an old airplane wreck.

The above gives you an idea of how some young people feel about the backcountry. On occasion, you'll also see individuals who carry sacks and pick up garbage left by careless fishermen or hunters. (Hikers generally know better than to litter.) It is true that if you try to bury cans, paper, or plastic, the animals may dig them up and scatter them. Carry it all back to civilization. After all, that's where it came from. To be sure, some of the sins add up. Like carving your name onto trees. Painting trailside rocks. Defacing trail signs. Tossing tabs from pop-top beverage cans into streams and lakes. Carelessly discarding foil-wrap and tear-off parts of instant snapshot film.

Environmental awareness means that you won't do any of those things. Here are some additional wilderness rules for backpackers:

- Leave wildflowers for the next person to enjoy and don't pull out ferns or cut trees.
- Forget about taking the family dog. Dogs scare wildlife.

- Don't contaminate the streams or lakes. Someone may need to drink this water.
- Conservation–don't cut across the switchbacks. They are constructed so as to handle rain runoff, and cutting the switchbacks starts erosion.
- Use existing fire sites whenever possible. If you camp where no one has been before, build a small fireplace. Never start fires near trees or on meadows, in your tent; don't place a fire against a log or back rock. *Never leave a fire unattended!* When breaking camp, drown the flames or cinders completely, stir, and drown again until the ashes are cold to the touch. Bury ashes and charcoal. Cover all traces. Except in well-established camps, return the rocks to their natural positions.

WHERE TO GO: PICKING YOUR MOUNTAINS

Where do you backpack? There are 10,000,000 acres of United States wilderness areas. Nine million acres of land in our national monuments. You can backpack in the depths of our national parks, in state parks, in America's national forests, in state forests, on private lands.

If your parents take you on a backpacking vacation to the mountains, you'll want to know something about the major mountain chains in North America. A little geography helps the backpacker. What are the differences in landscapes? The names of the peaks you can explore with a pack? How high are they?

Begin with the mountains of the eastern seaboard. They're more wooded than those of the West, and they're also much lower. The White Mountains, Green Mountains, and other eastern chains average 3,000 to 5,000-foot elevations. New England's ranges are worn and polished by successive ice movements which often left deep, steep ravines. Timberline ends at about 2,000 feet below the wind-blown summits. The popular 2,000-mile-long Appalachian Trail runs across the White Mountains of New Hampshire. En route to Maine, the trail also cuts through the undulating woodlands of Vermont's Green Mountains. (Shelters are provided, which lessens the burden on your back.) The Blue Mountains of Pennsylvania, the Berkshires of Massachussetts, Pennsylvania's Pocono Mountains, and New York's Adirondacks all attract backpackers. New York State's Mt. Marcy (5,347 feet) or further north, Quebec's Mont Tremblant (3,150 feet) serve young people well.

In the South, the Great Smoky Mountains National Park offers opportunities. In the Southwest, you can go backpacking in Arizona. Spring and late fall are the best times here for families. A few years ago, the sightseers only saw the Grand Canyon by automobile. Now some 12,000 travelers yearly take in the splendors by hiking into the Canyon and gazing up at the rim. Many of the visitors are backpackers.

Canadian backpackers are equally fortunate. The provinces of British Columbia or Alberta are full of exciting wilderness, and government agencies built trails in Quebec's

Boys learn to find their way in the wilderness. *(Outward Bound School)*

Laurentians, Saskatchewan's Meadow Lake Provincial Park, and Manitoba's Grass River National Park. Rural Ontario's "Bruce Trail" fetches backpacking youths as do the trails in many other provinces.

The summer months can be a delight in the Rocky Mountains. They stretch for more than 3,300 miles from Northern Alaska to Mexico. Their geographical importance is underlined by acting as watersheds and chutes for rivers. Recreation? You can still backpack into the wrinkled Sawtooth Ranges of Idaho without meeting too many people. You'll find trails galore, waterfalls, and wild Alpine lakes filled with trout. The Lost River Range includes Mt. Borah, Idaho's highest peak. Montana's portion of the Rockies also attracts young people. The late Chet Huntley, a Montanan by birth, outdoorsman and hiker, loved his state's High Country. He worshipped the Rockies in his neck of the woods: Granite Peak, Tumble Mountain, Lone Mountain. Huntley once said it beautifully, "A mountain range is forever so magnificently and perfectly based, all in proportion, its shoulders and snow crown in harmony with the gently ascending foothills. From a distance, the timber belt is a band of color, a great blue-green gash, and soaring out of it, the craggy slabs and domes and spires."

Wyoming's Wind River Range offers great appeal–several thousand square miles with only a few communities.

In certain sections, the Colorado Rockies are also thinly populated and unvisited. You may choose among 55 peaks of over 14,000 feet and 1,000 higher than 10,000 feet. In southern Colorado the Sangre de Cristo Range has some 42 peaks exceeding 13,000 feet, yet hardly any people. This makes for wonderful wilderness backpacking.

Colorado's most famous peaks are Pike's Peak (near Colorado Springs), Long's Peak (Estes Park), and the Maroon Bells (Aspen). A midwestern teenage boy described the sight of the Maroon Bells in a letter to his parents. He wrote: "A fantastic range of towering peaks inhabits what seems to be the rest of the world. . . . They just sit there and look at you like a bunch of nobles and you feel humble."

There are seldom such elevations or similar views to be had in the New Mexico or Utah section of the Rockies. Utah's Wasatch Range is handsome enough; Utah's highest peak is King's Mountain at 13,528 feet. Some of the state's canyons will startle you with their rock shapes and colors. New Mexico's Sangre de Cristos are not enormous. The state's Wheeler Peak doesn't reach Colorado heights, and most of the scenery is tamer than Colorado's. The soft brown colors and the gentle lines of the Santa Fe and Taos Mountains are something else again, offering great inspiration to painters.

The 430-mile-long Sierra Nevada can be found in California and Nevada, peaking to their highest point on Mt. Whitney (14,495 feet).

North of the Sierra, the Cascades hold their own court. The Cascade kingdom of high thrones, thick forests, and moist valleys extends seven hundred miles, all the way into Canada. The Pacific Northwest has great impact on young backpackers. Some of this magnificent country includes 14,162-foot Mt. Shasta, Mt. Adams, and other glacier-volcanoes.

SOME GROUPS THAT CAN TAKE YOU BACKPACKING

The Sierra Club, 530 Bush Street, San Francisco, CA 94108 (Family programs and junior backpackers.)

Sierra Club, 800 Second Avenue, New York, NY 10017 (Ages twelve and up.)

The Adirondack Forty-Sixers, Adirondack, NY 12808 (Takes guests on backpacking trips.)

Appalachian Mountain Club, 5 Joy Street, Boston, MA 02108

American Youth Hostels, Inc., Delaplane, VA 22025

The Wilderness Institute, Inc., P.O. Box 338, Bonners Ferry, ID 83805

"Skyline Trail Hikers Club," Box 5905, Calgary, Alberta, Canada (Organizes many outings for people of all ages.)

Northern Lights Alpine Recreation, Box 399, Invermere, British Columbia, Canada, VOA 1KO (Includes outings to glaciers.)

Backpacking With Barrow, Shirley M. Barrow, Outfitter, P.O. Box 183, Whitefish, MT 59937 (All ages.)

Mansfield Boys Camps, Box 1214, Steamboat Springs, CO 80477 (Ages nine–twelve.)

Rocky Mountain Backpack Tours, P.O. Box 2781, Evergreen, CO 80459 (Families.)

Colorado Mountain Club, 2530 West Alameda Avenue, Denver, CO 80219

USEFUL ADDRESSES FOR MORE INFORMATION

National Park Service, Department of the Interior, Washington, DC 20240

The American Forestry Association, 1219 18th Street, N.W., Washington, DC 20036 (Has outdoor programs.)

Wilderness Society, 729 15th Street, Washington, DC 20005

United States Forest Service, S.W., Washington, DC 20250

National Recreation and Park Association, 1700 Pennsylvania Avenue, Washington, DC 20006

Bruce Trail Association, 33 Hardale Crescent, Hamilton, Ontario, Canada

CHAPTER 4

The Novice Climber

ROCK CLIMBING: WHAT IT REALLY FEELS LIKE

It is early morning. The breeze touches your nostrils, cools your brow, stirs your mind. You're alive. You have space: the mountain flows up into the sky. You're with three other people—two girls and a boy—all your own age.

The rocks are ready for you. A companion uncoils the rope. You allow yourselves a standing pause. The New England highway that brought you is already a silver wire far beneath you. Toy cars streak along down there. You don't envy the drivers, all cooped up while you're free to move. "Let's go!"

This is mountaineering.

And this: You're in motion, searching and finding those holds for hand and feet, reaching high up, leaning out, keeping your balance. You see chipmunks darting from ground that slopes down the flanks of the rock. A few harmless lizards peek out of cracks. The summit seems cemented against a blue sky. Safely tied to a rope, it is good to touch the warm stone, claw it, inch up on it, and hold onto it. Rock climbing is more than a sport; you may call it also an embrace with the earth. A sheer wall. Smiles of encouragement, then ledges for only two at a time. Higher up, everything is more intense: the sun fiercer, the walls more dizzying, the views more stunning. You're aware of your body, and all the while, your heart pounds.

THE CLIMBING MYSTIQUE: WHY THEY DO IT

Ask one hundred young people why they go to climbing camps, why they talk their parents into taking them into the high country for rock climbing. You'll get a dozen answers.

First of all, as we've seen, climbing brings people closer together. Because we're responsible for the lives of each other, we can also become better friends. You truly get companionship. Woodrow Wilson Sayre, an American philosopher, once put it this way: "Real friendship is increasingly difficult," he said. "We hurry so much, we move to another town, we juggle a hundred responsibilities. How often do we see our best friends? Once a week? Once a month? Less than that? If we hardly see them, can we really share joy and tragedy with them? I think people are made for a deeper sort of friendship. If they miss it, they miss something very important in life. They are made for the close warmth tested in the mountains."

When you ask other young people why they started rock climbing, you get responses like: "I like to fool around with hardware." "For the action, man." "My boyfriend talked me into it." "I wanted to see if I had the guts." One well-known guide has said that he is only fully alive in the mountains. Other rock climbers do it because they want to escape from the soft city life, to test themselves, to be free, to get some exercise. You drink, and water never tasted so sweet. Food goes down remarkably well after the day's clambering across rocks and ice fields.

Climbers also mention the sheer beauty of the mountains. The colors change all the time. A sudden light beam can brighten a meadow and sharpen the crests above. Each trip is new. You will climb peaks in delightfully soft sunshine or under ultraviolet rays that tan even the palest faces.

John Muir, the California naturalist, may have expressed it best of all: "Climb the mountains!" he wrote. "Nature's peace will flow into you like sunshine flows into trees. The winds will flow their own freshness into you . . . while cares drop off like autumn leaves."

SOME REQUIREMENTS

Strange as it may seem, rock climbing isn't a matter of strength; that's why some teenage girls are sometimes better than boys their age. Muscle has little to do with your performance on the wall. Any normally fit person can learn to climb. You're no exception if you happen to live in the flatland and get to the mountains only once a year.

What are the requirements then? Call it your inner attitude. Rock climbing takes courage and self-confidence. You must be able to move freely and without fear 10, 20, 50, or more meters above the ground.

This fearlessness can be difficult to achieve during the first

Author shows an easy climb. Note rope for safety.

few climbing hours. Some young climbers have no fear at all; others overcome their anxiety almost at once.

The rest is a sense of balance, the common sense not to get in over your head, and technique. Anyone who is somewhat athletic can actually learn the basic rope techniques in a couple of days. According to one mountain guide, "It's the soul that counts, not the body."

Most young people climb with ease. "It's a natural instinct," says a former member of an American Everest expedition. "An infant already wants to climb out of the playpen!" Gaston Rebuffat, one of Europe's most celebrated guides and Alpinists, has stated: "Every youngster has a talent for climbing. Don't they all climb windowsills and trees!"

A mature attitude counts greatly. Do you consider yourself safety-conscious? Do you think of the whole team? Can you endure some physical strain? If so, you become a good candidate for technical rock climbing.

There is another side. Some people never get used to heights and quickly drop out. Others find the mental strain of searching for correct handholds and footholds almost unbearable. Still others don't like the military tone while on a rope or don't like the uptightness of some climbing situations. Climbing is not everyone's cup of rock. Many people prefer hiking.

GETTING STARTED

How do you get started in mountaineering? First of all, look up the address of the nearest mountain club, guide, and program at the end of this chapter. Consider special summer camps or a YMCA. You can also join one of the country's many mountain clubs and thus climb as part of a supervised junior group. Several of these clubs have special junior schools. For those in their late teens, the best rock climbing courses are held by the Outward Bound schools in several parts of the United States. Some national park guide services teach young persons to scale rocks.

Mountain climbing lessons mean learning the ropes first! *(Colorado Mountain Club)*

Whether you join an organized group or go with friends, you're likely to begin with a hike. Stick to the trails at first, then try some ramp-like rocks that you can *walk* up. Watch others as they scale more difficult terrain such as granite walls, "chimneys," and overhanging boulders. You can see climbing exhibitions in most mountainous states. Outside Colorado Springs, for instance, there are daily summer demonstrations by army mountaineers. If this whets your appetite, you may be all set to take climbing lessons in a national park or to join one of the mountaineering schools that are part of many mountain clubs. (A few high schools also have special summer and fall programs.)

You can also get started by going with an experienced friend. Make sure to ask if he or she has climbed for a long time. (One or two outings are never enough.) Experts agree that a little rock scrambling of an hour or two makes a good beginning.

Try your natural skills on a boulder first. It needn't be very large; it could be, for instance, just two or three times your own height. Look for footholds and handholds. Move up carefully. If you should fall, you won't have far to go. A large boulder gives you a chance to test your leader and your rope.

How about a more ambitious trip that takes half a day? Work up to it. Don't strain yourself. Wait for overnight climbs until you're at least twelve years old or older. Most climbing schools will seldom take you on difficult routes until you're in your teens. Naturally, there are exceptions, such as people who were born (and live) in the high country or are extremely developed.

Even on easier rock faces, good climbers pick every step with care. They think and plan every move. Each foothold

This photo shows the "rappel"; it is easy to learn in a climbing school. *(Curtis Casewit)*

"Rappel!" *(Colorado Outward Bound, Inc.)*

and handhold must be tested to see if it is safe or if rock could break loose. You try not to slip; at all times, you must have three points of contact with the mountain. The contact can be two hands and one foot or one hand and two feet. (Knees are never used.) Skilled climbers never grip bushes, small trees, or other "vegetable holds" because plants seldom have deep roots in stone.

The proper climbing position distinguishes the expert from the novice. New climbers often lean into the mountain, hugging it. You are safest by keeping your upper body away from the rock. And you always look up.

Seasoned mountaineers bring a rope for safer ascents and descents. Once you know how to use it, a rope becomes a link to your climbing partners. It takes time to understand and practice the needed rope knots, and you will need instruction in the art of anchoring yourself safely to "belay" the rest of your roped clan. ("Belaying" means you're the anchor person for other climbers.) Technique is also required for the exciting "rappel." This maneuver allows you to back down the steepest mountain face in record time, thanks to a nylon rope.

Only the first step over the void takes courage; the rest of the downward journey is easy in the company of pros. But some youngsters–and most adults–have trouble with that first step. They have butterflies in their stomachs. How do professional climbing instructors teach you? Here's what one well-known climbing teacher says: "It's not hard to get the kids over the rim. Especially if I let a girl go off first. She may act scared. Maybe even *be* scared. But after I show how it's done–she'll rappel. Of course, the boys don't want to look like cowards. So they follow. Some of these young climbers are naturals, anyway. A few of them catch on rapidly. And get a kick out of it."

It's always essential to assemble at least four people. If they want to move fast, they form two rope teams of two people each. (A two-person party is about three times as fast as a three-person party.) It's logical that the weaker individual is always behind the stronger one on the way up and ahead on the way down. It also makes sense that when there are four people, the two strong climbers should not be together. This would result in letting the two weak ones fend for themselves on another rope. The rope is only a safety device; it is never used hand over hand.

HOW TO OUTFIT YOURSELF

A climber should take no chances. Begin with clothes. Bring a pair of comfortable slacks instead of the too-tight jeans. You need freedom of motion. Shorts are okay, although they can mean scraped legs.

A waterproof parka (or windbreaker) is essential because temperatures can drop unexpectedly. The first mountain rain tests a parka's quality. An experiment-minded Illinois girl put on the new parka at home and stepped under the shower. After fifteen minutes, she was still dry. United States Army testing goes even further. Soldiers step on treadmills and under sprinklers of special "Rain Rooms." The test includes getting wet from perspiration inside and water outside. Warm socks and first-class boots with Vibram lug soles are important. A flannel shirt and a spare sweater also help.

The leader usually provides the rope, which may be anywhere from 120 to 150 feet long, can stand 3,000-pound tension, and does much better than a clothesline.

All mountaineering schools supply the ropes. The modern synthetic article is sturdy and durable. (An imported German Perlon rope can actually hold some 5,000 pounds before it breaks.) New climbers are warned right away that they must treat the strands with care. One brand actually comes with a label that reads: "If anyone steps on it, even your best friend, bash him!" Too much abuse causes the synthetic fibers to weaken and break. A climbing rope has only a limited span of mountain life, too, and must be replaced periodically.

Along with the rope, climbers use various pieces of hardware that are usually carried by the leader or guide. These

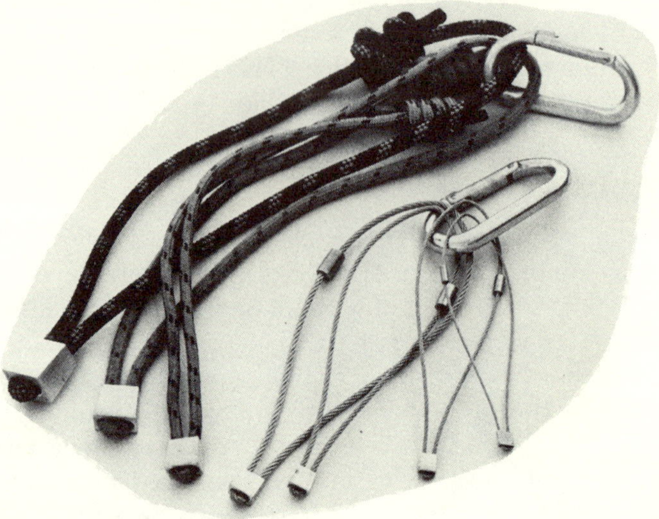

Up-to-date hardware is essential for safe climbing. *(Foto Frost, Ventura, CA)*

Hardware like this is used by young climbers because the climbers of today no longer believe in "nailing." The piece can later be removed. *(Forest Mountaineering)*

items include chocks (removable metal spikes of various shapes) and oval-shaped rings (called carabiners or "snap links").

CAUTION . . . A MUST

Mountains do not forgive our errors. Rock climbers are in the first line of fire. Caution is not only important but a must. First of all, *never* climb alone. For safety's sake, there must always be several climbers. A group's lack of experience and lack of equipment are both dangerous.

Your safety depends on your leader. If he is reckless, overconfident, or inexperienced, you're in for trouble. He better know all about equipment, routes, weather.

All leaders and knowledgeable mountaineers are aware of objective dangers. One of these is slippery wet rock. (Turn back on a rainy day.) Falling rock represents a common danger, too. If the leader should dislodge even a pebble, he'll shout: "Rock!" Needless to say, climbers should never toss objects from a summit.

Mountaineers stick to the rule of coming down the same way they went up, unless they know a peak intimately. The untried side of a mountain may be too steep. A few years ago, a group of Colorado teenagers started out too late in the day. Operating without a plan, they reached a difficult summit near Aspen, just as the sun went down behind the Rockies. The boys tried to find a shortcut, and all but one fell down the precipice. Climbing in the darkness is not a smart idea, either.

BASIC SAFETY RULES

Some of the most important rules have been summed up by the junior chapter of the Colorado Mountain Club. Consider the following items:

1. Travel with a minimum party of four. If a member of the party is injured, one person can stay with that person while the other two, safeguarding each other, go for help.

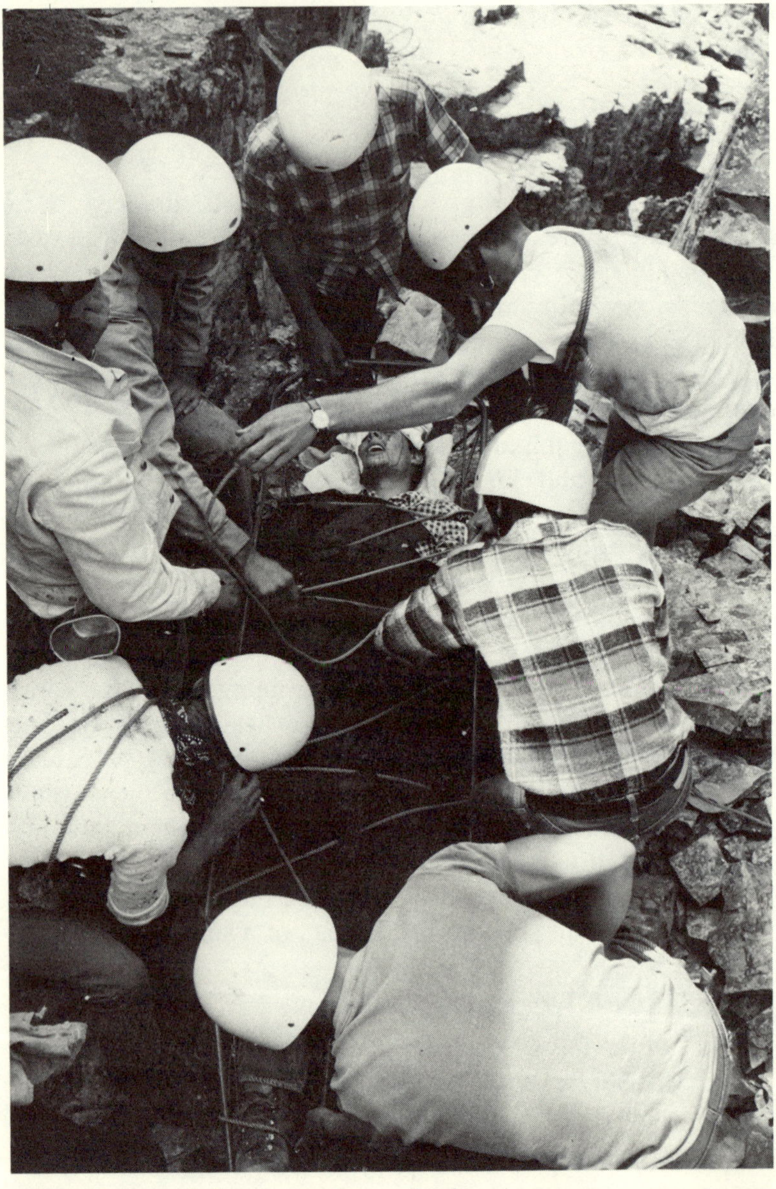

This climber obviously made a mistake. A rescue group at once goes into action. *(Colorado Outward Bound, Inc.)*

2. Obey the trip leader. The trip leader should be in complete charge of the party. He/she can ask for opinion, but the leader makes the final decision.
3. Keep the party together. In this way the party members can keep track of each other and render assistance when required.
4. Realize the party's limitations. Never venture beyond the knowledge or ability of the group. Choose a route and a point for turning back that are within the limits of all climbers.
5. Follow the rules of sound mountaineering. These rules are set forth in climbing textbooks.
6. Register your trip. To insure assistance in event of an accident, you should register the trip in one or all of the following ways: A responsible friend or member of your family who knows what to do if the party does not return as planned. The local Ranger Station in the area of your trip. A mountain rescue unit. Let them know
   a. The name, address, and phone number of each climber.
   b. What you are climbing.
   c. The route and secondary route of ascent and descent.
   d. Your approximate time of return.
   e. The approximate time to go looking for your group if you are overdue (usually noon the following day).
   f. The description and license number of your car. Be sure to sign out on all climbing registers or check out with the proper persons upon your safe return.

By and large, mountaineering is not as dangerous as it sounds. Fatalities are rare, and according to the American Alpine Club figures, there are less than one hundred major accidents per year.

WHERE TO CLIMB AND SOME USEFUL ADDRESSES

North American youngsters have more opportunities than they suspect. Begin in Maine, where Mt. Katahdin provides climbers with several thousand feet of granite. (One approaches the 5,267-foot Maine champion from Millinocket.) The Mt. Washington region, near Franconia, New Hampshire, attracts climbers. There are also some satisfactory cliffs in New York's Lake Placid area, in the Hudson Valley, and in the Shawangunk Mountains.

Climbing activity booms all over the world. Young men and women not only scale the Rocky Mountains, the Sierras, and the Alps, but also the Romsdal Range of Norway, the Spanish Pyrenees, the Italian Apennines, the Yugoslav Karawanken.

In this country mountaineering clubs do an excellent job. For example, the "Mountaineers," a large group in Seattle, Washington, has special courses for novice climbers in the Cascades. People start with lectures, then go to practice sessions in nearby mountains, and finally move up to more difficult and very safe climbs. The Appalachian Mountain Club offers some junior climbing in the East. Live in Iowa City? The Iowa Mountaineers are an active group. Honolulu? There's the Hawaiian Trail and Mountain Club.

SOME USEFUL CLUBS FOR YOUNG CLIMBERS

Appalachian Mountain Club, 5 Joy Street, Boston, MA 02108

Berkeley Hiking Club, Box 147, Berkeley, CA 94701

Colorado Mountain Club, 2530 West Alameda, Denver, CO 80219

Hawaiian Trail and Mountain Club, P.O. Box 2238, Honolulu, HI 96814

Iowa Mountaineers, P.O. Box 163, Iowa City, IA 52242

The Mountaineers, Box 122, Seattle, WA 98111

The Sierra Club, 1050 Mills Tower, San Francisco, CA 94104

SOME GUIDE SERVICES AND SCHOOLS

Teton Mountain Guide Service & School of American Mountaineering, Moose Post Office, Moose, WY 83012

Mount Rainier Guide Service, 1525 11th Avenue, Seattle, WA 98122

Rocky Mountain Climbing School, Estes Park, CO 80517

Rocky Mountain Guides Ltd., P.O. Box 1660, Banff, Alberta, Canada

Lassen Venture, 3272 Alpine Road, Menlo Park, CA 94025

The Blazed Trail/Climbing School, 360 Madison Avenue, New York, NY 10017 (Must have permission from parents.)

Outward Bound, Inc., 165 West Putnam Avenue, Greenwich, CT 06830 (Late teens only.)

CHAPTER 5

Advanced Climbing in Rock and Ice

WHO BECOMES AN ADVANCED CLIMBER?

When you started to climb, you no doubt began by walking up some easy rocks in an upright position. Later, you did some steeper rock scrambling. It was still simple and safe enough, and your party didn't require a rope. You learned to use your hands and feet for balance, to feel sure on boulders and easy rocks. Perhaps you graduated to Class III climbing, which already took you to steeper terrain, still without equipment.

You become an advanced technical climber when you begin to tackle faces that lean about 60 degrees to vertical. At this point, your belay (which we discussed in the previous chapter) has to be one hundred percent safe, and you'll have to know how to deal with hardware.

Practice in Class IV climbing plus experience in all kinds of terrain contribute to an individual's confidence. The ambitious young Class V climber gradually advances to Class VI. At this point, first-rate leadership, good health, self-confidence, and endurance become essential. The climber should be accustomed to the "exposure" of steep drop-offs. A good attitude, mechanical aptitude, a sense for route finding, and weather knowledge now pay off.

Some of the Class VI types manage to scale rocks with very few handholds. Youth presents no problems; you'll see first-class climbers at age twelve, thirteen, fourteen.

Most of these rock artists either live near high mountains or travel there at least once a year. Willing parents are useful to develop a climber. Practice counts.

Sheer intelligence and talent also help. Many young experts regard rock formations as puzzles and technical challenges. They live for the texture and grain of a cliff. They don't mind the scratches or gashes on their arms and legs, or rocks that almost cause frostbite or get griddle-hot. These climbers wait with unbelievable patience on some narrow shelf, broiling in the heat until the belayer gives the signal to climb the next pitch.

There are people who specialize in rock, while others find happiness only on steep ice walls, or on long-crevassed glaciers that require the greatest stamina.

Money can be immaterial to mountaineers. During the 1850s an English mountaineer was asked whether the mountain ever repaid him for the efforts. The Englishman replied that the labor itself was part of the pleasure. Another explained that he was rewarded, "with the delightful discovery that man is the sum of his own simple powers." The attitude has changed little even now. One of the best young American elite climbers completed a hair-raising rescue mission. A magazine offered him a big sum for the exploit. The American shook his head. "I like to climb," he said. "Isn't that enough?" Unlike the leading modern ski racers, the great climbers don't have tie-ins with products. They don't commercialize mountaineering.

Most young elite climbers also help others as part of rescue teams or as instructors. Advanced climbing no doubt builds character. These people can be counted on. They're reliable.

SOME TECHNICAL POINTS

Remember that in each party, only one person does the climbing at a time. Some Yosemite climbers only gain 70 feet in five hours. There doesn't seem to be much drama here.

Only precision and caution and labor. In fact, advanced rock enthusiasts don't worry about how they look to others. They care only about the safety of their team. Every step is measured. Bill Forrest, well known for first ascents, puts it this way: "We climb with hands and heart, head and feet; these are primary–equipment is secondary. A climber holds life in his own hands; he must live by his own decisions."

These realities are the heart of climbing adventures where your own decisiveness brings life into sharper focus. Lured by the hunch that you can make the route go right or left, around or up, you try with your body what your eye and mind have seen. And when, with a succession of rhythmic pulls and pushes and self-control, you succeed in surmounting those difficulties, you are happy.

The climbing sense generally develops only after you gain a lot of experience. It can be gotten with others your age who have teamed up with experts for a long time. Or you can take a course in advanced techniques. What do they teach?

A typical rock climbing school insists on two important lessons. An instructor explains: "Belaying the leader–this lesson is devoted to the leader belays. We will practice the leader belay in realistic climbing situations, using up-to-date techniques. The use of belaying devices will be discussed. The student will set up belays and place his own anchors. There will be further practice in free-climbing. Leading the rope–this lesson is concerned with techniques of leading and will introduce the student to sling and nut placement for leader protection. The student will climb second over pitches upon which the various protection devices will be demonstrated. Although the proper use of hardware will be shown, the emphasis in this lesson will be upon using 'natural' protection techniques and 'clean climbing.' "

Your next step will be the vital technique of the "direct aid;" it allows you to reach steep rock that is otherwise unclimbable. The use of ropes, hardware, and other gear makes it

Difficult overhanging rocks like these require some experience. Don't attempt a climb into tricky terrain on your first outing. *(John Bryan)*

possible to brave thousands of feet, even to surmount overhanging rock, and to come down safely again.

Removable "nuts" or "chocks" are wedged into cracks; these anchors can be connected to the rope via carabiners. These oval pieces can stand great stresses; in fact, "biners" have been tested for weights of 3,000 pounds and more. Naturally, every intermediate and advanced climber must be capable of making safe rope knots for roping up or tying in. Leaders and instructors have their own preferences, of course, but you'll be expected to do your own rope knotting. Likewise, you're expected to place hardware in cracks.

An advanced climber usually masters all the techniques. You will first exhaust the natural possibilities. If the wall cannot be taken any other way, even the most conservation-conscious mountaineer must use other hardware, such as pitons (steel spikes). This happens most frequently when the climber faces a major rock outcrop, known as an "overhang."

In other cases, pitons must be used to allow a quick descent in bad weather. Advanced climbers can actually scale almost any surface they please and reach great heights by means of special gear. This includes "etriers" (rope ladders).

At one point in mountaineering history, some direct-aid specialists were called "rock engineers." This was at a time of fewer climbers and more unclimbed terrain. For some people, the gadgetry itself was the thing. Rock engineers would arrive heavily armed against their targets. Packs full of pitons and etriers were not enough; these climbers would also attack walls with large hammers and even drills or bolts. A minority would pound big, blade-like "bongs" into cracks. Two decades ago, even well-known international names liked to "hammer-and-nail" their way up a mountain face. Some of the soft hardware couldn't be pulled out again. The pitons had to be left behind in wind, rain, and snow, later rusting away. The metal became an eyesore.

Fortunately for the environment, the rope has swung in the other direction. The new climbers refuse to destroy rock faces with pitons or the even larger bolts. Some climbers do not even dare to use chalk for their palms because it rubs off on rock. They never leave empty cans on ledges, or toss things into valleys. They'll make an occasional stop to admire the view. And they're often familiar with the geology of the mountains they climb.

KNOWING DIFFERENT ROCK

Which rock is safest? Which type can crumble? Is it possible to find different layers on one mountain? Advanced rock enthusiasts can answer questions like these. The climbers generally know what they're facing. Granite is one of the best (and best known) rocks for climbers. Gneiss and schist can crumble.

To the climbing geologist, there is not only the mountain's granite and other rocks, but there are also the rock-forming minerals like quartz, feldspars, and calcites. There are metamorphic rocks that changed their composition because of temperature extremes and other factors. A mountain can consist of igneous rocks, which were once part of fiery volcanoes. Sandstone, such as you find in Colorado, has the disadvantage of fewer cracks for handholds or footholds.

Most of the world's mountain ranges are made up of "sandwiches." It all goes back to an often tumultuous geological history. Geologists call the Rockies complicated ranges with intricate patterns of folded rock strata, a complex pyramid of several kinds of rocks. Some of these patterns can be visible to anyone. Wyoming's Mt. Moran, one of the Grand Tetons, for example, features a streak of black stone on its face. This is of volcanic origin; it was formed by hot lava that boiled its way into a long, cold crack.

THE ADVANCED CLIMBER AND SAFETY

It is the mark of the better climber to be doubly safety-conscious. Caution always improves your chances to come down safely. According to the American Alpine Club, 80 percent of all mountaineering accidents in the United States are caused by human failure such as exceeding one's abilities, climbing when exhausted, pushing on in bad weather, running out of food, climbing in unknown terrain without preparation, or having no regard for the weather. No one should ignore the threat of storms. Experience means anticipating a mountain's moods, the sudden cold and lightning, the snow avalanche, the cascade of rock. The expert knows what to do about these real dangers.

Good equipment nowadays includes the protection of your head by means of a hard hat. Ropes must be new or undamaged. Hardware should be tested before use and cannot be bought secondhand. The climbing language must remain uniform, too. It is simple enough: You will shout to your climbing partner, who is belaying (securing) you, "Climbing!" He replies, "Climb!" and you will now start up the

Few young climbers will have to perform feats like this one. But it can be learned. *(U.S. Army)*

rock. "Belay on" means that a belay is ready for you. "Off belay" signals the end of the belay. If you touch bottom after a rappel, it's "Off rappel." "Rock!" alerts others about a dislodged piece of rock, giving them a chance to get out of the way. "Falling!" tells your leader just that.

Most falls are harmless. Good technique means safe chocks or pitons. Nevertheless, despite every precaution, dangers still exist. That's why you (or your parents) have to sign a legal release before you can enroll in a climbing school. The document reads as follows:

> I fully realize that mountaineering can be a dangerous sport; even experts following the best of safety and climbing techniques are sometimes injured. Such risks as lightning, avalanches, falling rocks, ropes breaking, pitons failing or pulling out, carabiners breaking, hands or feet slipping, too much cold or too much heat are some of the risks that I acknowledge exist.

To prevent accidents, the national parks do not permit solo climbing. The equipment of your party will be inspected; in fact, you must obtain permission to climb. This is a good idea. In mountaineering history, there are a number of examples of people taking on high mountains without adequate gear. One example was the first attempt to reach the top of Switzerland's Matterhorn. The climbers had almost gotten to the summit when their rope broke. Edward Whymper, the British leader, survived the fall. But his warning remains important. "There have been joys too great to be described in words, and there have been griefs upon which I have not dared to dwell," Whymper wrote. "With these in mind I say, 'Climb if you will, but remember that courage and strength are nought without prudence, and that a momentary negligency may destroy the happiness of a lifetime. Do nothing in haste; look well to each step; and from the beginning think what may be the end.' "

CLIMBING IN ICE

It is not impossible that someday you'll be exploring in eternal ice regions. You may be visiting Mt. Rainier near Seattle, for instance, which is a big glacier that demands special techniques. Or you may join a group to scale the Tetons in winter. Or even travel to Europe, where numerous glaciers attract climbers. Before you can join a snow and ice workshop, you'll have to rent an ice axe, which is used both as a safety device and as a tool on ice climbs. You'll need to rent (or buy) crampons; these spikes allow you to tread safely on ice. A helmet is generally required, too.

What is a typical ice workshop like? What do you learn? The description from a Wyoming guide service tells you more about two summer programs. Snow and ice seminar—this four-day seminar provides a basic orientation to snow and ice technique. A day is spent in approach to the climbing area, a day of technical snow, and a day of technical ice, returning the day following. An excellent foundation in Alpine technique.

Ice seminar—the four-day ice seminar is designed for those already possessing snow and rock competence who wish to learn the fine points of technical ice climbing and participate in a long classic ice climb. This seminar requires reasonable physical condition.

Once more, seasoned leadership becomes vital. The leader will be responsible to test the ice with the axe. The leader teaches you how to walk with crampons and how to stop from falling down a glacier by means of an ice axe "self-arrest." (If you should slide, you must at once dig into the ice with your axe and break the fall.) Advanced students learn about handling ropes and get to practice with more advanced equipment such as ice screws and stake-like anchors known as "pickets." The scaling of ice walls is now possible. All the while, safe belays are taught, too.

Safety comes in numbers of two or more. On a snow-covered glacier, you need at least three on the rope. You can overdo it, of course. A crazy story still makes the rounds in the Cascades.

One summer, seventeen people plodded up the not-to-difficult face of one glacier. The mishap happened near the summit. One fellow slipped and down came all sixteen others. Into a crevasse. All on top of each other, crampons and all. No one was killed, although several of the mad-hatter crew required stitches.

WEATHER FACTORS

Much always depends on good weather. A summer blizzard in the high mountains can be dangerous, especially if you lack warm clothing. Even well-equipped groups often turn back and return to the valley. Certain regions of North America have severe weather even in summer.

One example is Mt. McKinley in Alaska. A climber should not expect any summer favors from the frigid colossus of Mt. McKinley. With measurements of 20,320 feet (from a base of 1,000 feet!), McKinley represents the ceiling of North America. One must remember that the peak juts into the Alaskan sky just 250 miles south of the Arctic Circle. Summer daylight extends for nearly twenty-four hours, and on McKinley's upper reaches, snow falls every month. During most of the year, the cover reaches down to 4,000 feet. Winter Alpinists figure on temperatures of fifty degrees below zero.

Alaskan blizzards create havoc in spring, too, and even a light wind can drive the thermometer down to below thirty. The National Park Rangers tell all prospective McKinley visitors to "expect arctic conditions." The danger of freezing one's face, hands, and feet is always present. Prolonged storms often force groups to hole-up for several days in tents or snow caves. Bradford Washburn, a long-time expert on Alaska, speaks of furious June winds that can accelerate to one hundred miles an hour. "These winds make the peak a veritable inferno of evil weather," says Washburn, who once spent eighty-nine days on McKinley. Only five days were clear. Washburn gives many reasons for these bad climatic conditions. For one thing, the lone Mt. McKinley gets hit by all coastal storms. For another, McKinley, like other high peaks, makes its own storms. An interplay of warmer valley air, moisture, and summit winds creates the typical cloudcaps. The cloud mass expands, and within fifteen to twenty minutes, develops into a localized blizzard.

The hovering white masses are characteristic for the giants of the Pacific Northwest and the Rockies as well. In the valleys, meanwhile, the sun may shine. The opposite can also be true. One day three U.S. climbers reached the McKinley summit and returned through fine weather to the base of the mountain. It was here that they were caught in a five-day storm that pinned the men into their tents. It would have been unthinkable to attempt the long march back to civilization just then.

GLACIER KNOWLEDGE

Just as you should know a little about some of the rocks, you'll be wise to gain some knowledge about glaciers.

A genuine glacier always moves at some period or is still

in motion. The surface may consist of hard ice or crusted snow or both. A glacier can glare like a thousand sun-reflecting mirrors. Big glaciers may be knifed by short, dark lines of crevasses (or fissures) caused by stresses and ice movements.

Do most glaciers get bigger or smaller? Their advance or retreat actually depends on the amount of yearly moisture and on temperature. Some glaciers move as much as 600 miles a year. One of the most interesting surveys was made by a team of scientists in Alaska over a twenty-five-year period. Of two hundred Alaskan glaciers, about 60 percent of the glaciers shrank; about 17 percent advanced, and the rest "held their own."

Graphs show that the ice can surge forward more at certain times than at others. Some scientists calculated that a mountain can "stampede" 2 feet per hour at its edges and twice as fast in midstream. In the Rockies, glacial flow is usually more modest; the Arapahoe Glacier (the water source for the city of Boulder, Colorado) crawls along at a rate of only 11 to 27 feet a year. Colorado's biggest glacier reaches a maximum thickness of a mere 500 feet. (Arapahoe's average is about 100 feet, not much compared to the Antarctic.) Arapahoe Glacier's major crevasse, known as the "bergschrund," marks the area where the glacier broke away from the top of the mountain and slid downward. Each season's 25 to 35 feet of snowfall accumulates in tidy white layers that are in turn separated by thin brown lines. The lines give you some clue to a glacier's age, like the rings inside a tree. Apart from the old snow layers, glaciers may also have dramatic overhanging cornices, or ice lips. They're the work of heat and wind, melting, and air currents.

Should one automatically call a year-round snow pinnacle a "glacier"? Not at all. Colorado's St. Mary's Glacier, for instance, is not a real glacier, despite its name or snow cover. St. Mary's, like other such peaks in the West, serves year-round skiers during the early mornings before the snow turns soft.

CHAPTER 6

Cross-Country Skiing

THE QUIET PLEASURES OF THE SKI TOUR

It is a lovely afternoon. On the hillside above your town, the snow sparkles. The sky is clear. You're on cross-country skis that slide easily up toward a forest glade. Two companions are ahead of you; you follow their twin tracks.

You can't hear them. There is silence except for the purr of your light wood skis against the snow. Your ski poles whisper as you move up and up. Deep breaths! Single-file under the winter sun, with your friends always in sight.

So far, no one has spoken. But the others—a girl and a boy—now stop among the white-pillowed cottonwood trees and wait for you. Although the altitude gain was only a few hundred feet, the town below looks different. More compact. More orderly. You see your school in a mauve haze. You see your own tracks carved into the meadow.

You're on a one-hour cross-country ski tour, a quiet pleasure that will acquaint you with the rolling midwestern country where you make your home.

Ski touring, or cross-country skiing (which means the same thing), puts us in touch with Mother Nature. As "XC" skiers, we move slowly enough for our eyes to take in the imprint left by animals. We can study the bark of trees, the needles of conifers, the leafless bushes already preparing for spring.

The purity of the cross-country experience is shown in this photo. *(Vail, CO)*

Here is a mountain sport that actually requires no mountains; so long as there are a few inches of snow, you can tour anywhere in the flat farm country. XC works fine on level ground. If you live in a large city, you can take your cross-country skis to a football field or to the nearest park and soon make tracks.

Here's a sport that can be enjoyed by healthy youngsters willing to try it. Farm meadows, golf courses, unplowed country roads, bicycle and bridle paths, hiking trails, logging roads, frozen lakes with a snow cover of only two inches–all serve the ski tourer.

Hills make the ski tour more interesting, more challenging. Elevations? Never mind; the gentlest, nearest ranges will do. Young midwesterners thus discover the same XC joys in Michigan or Wisconsin as they would in the Rockies. The mildly undulating terrain of Kansas, Texas, or Ontario will do, along with the flatlands of other states or the Canadian provinces.

On other occasions, and in other areas, you can examine the tracks of animals. Snowshoe rabbits, deer, or elk often roam the land in winter. As a cross-country skier, you'll be reminded of their presence.

MORE REASONS TO TRY IT

If you limit touring to flat or gently sloping terrain, the sport requires neither courage nor much effort. The skis weigh little. Your boots are light. The motion is natural. Compare it to a gentle winter hike, if you wish, and bear in mind that ski touring need not be competitive. Most young people do it for recreation.

Your output of strength is at first minimal; that is why this sport has taken hold among so many people of all ages–even small children like it. You do three to five miles per hour. The high-speed dangers of regular "Alpine" skiing are absent in ski touring, which is therefore much safer. Collisions are rare. So are broken legs.

To look good on a ski resort slope requires much instruction and practice; to look good on a cross-country trail takes only one day. The technique is fairly simple.

This Scandinavian sport can be learned with ease, even by high schoolers who are not especially fit. The entire family can go on a tour without much trouble.

Yet, XC is wonderful exercise. Your feet, ankles, lower legs, arms, forearms, and wrists are kept in constant motion. As you move on a trail, you improve posture and broaden your shoulders. Physicians point out that cross-country skiing quickens your breathing, increases your oxygen intake, and stimulates your circulation. The running, swinging, and bending means that you grow additional blood vessels. A one-hour session in the snow rouses a whole orchestra of small and large muscles, squeezing blood through your entire body. It's a means of toning up your physical machine.

Ski touring makes you feel better. Especially if you ski out in the country.

Cross-country skiers can get away from pollution. (They don't make pollution, like snowmobilers.) Call it an "ecological sport." Being so silent, the cross-country skier doesn't disturb the environment. "That's why the new generation gets turned on by the noiseless, fumeless way into the woods," says an official of the Ski Touring Council, which promotes XC in the United States. Touring also allows you to avoid the crowded ski resorts and the too-busy ski lifts. The sport is, therefore, much cheaper than "lift" skiing.

SKI TOURING FOR THE YOUNG NATURALIST: GETTING CLOSE TO THE COUNTRY

On a ski tour in the higher mountain ranges, you make fascinating discoveries. The summits are battlefields, where the cross-country tourer wanders among trees that seem to hug the ground or crouch behind boulders. These pines continue to exist despite severe mountaintop winds. The conifers are smaller than those in the valleys, and the branches may be shorter. On the summits the trunks will be bent and twisted, telling much about the snow loads. Long ago blizzards stripped their bark, and snow crystals sanded the wood. The sun bleaches it. But the sap still flows. Vegetation becomes more sparse on a summit, but many conifers survive. Some species–like the Bristlecone pine–live for several thousand years. The California cross-country skier can study these amazing trees.

Intriguingly, some mountain flora have adapted themselves well to the high country. Extremely cold temperatures can't hurt them. One of the best examples is lichen, a fine plant layer that belongs to the algae family. It takes many decades to grow but needs almost no nutrients. You'll see lichen sticking to dry or dewy surfaces of rocks. The plant reflects the colors of the seasons and the mountains, and you'll find lichen at many altitudes. In the meantime, some wildflowers sleep peacefully under the thickest snow cover, biding their time until spring. In Colorado, thousands of avalanche lilies push through the snow, surprising the cross-country explorer with their delicate (and edible) yellow petals.

EQUIPMENT

For ski touring you need no equipment except your own two feet and a pair of light boots, thin skis, and poles.

Think of used gear first. Look for it at Salvation Army stores, VFW, Goodwill stores, garage or yard sales, ski club "swaps." Or read the classified newspaper ads. A secondhand XC ski package should not put a dent in your allowance or savings.

Try the nearest ski shop or sporting goods store for rental of equipment. If you're at a small ski area, you can generally count on renting skis, boots, and poles by the day. The cost will be less than a dinner.

Fortunately, even new touring gear is inexpensive. At first, the lowest-priced wood skis should do, especially if you're still growing. Once you get turned on to touring, you can invest in better skis. These will be made of finer woods that consist of "sandwich" construction, or laminations. Modern fiberglass materials also add quality to cross-country skis, making them more durable. Keep in mind that a young novice does fine on the least costly skis; at first, most of your winter activity can take place in a local park or on farmland, where rugged skis are not necessary.

How long should your first pair of skis be? Stretch out your hand above your head; the tips of the skis ought to reach your palms or a little higher if you're still growing. In fact, an athletic young person seldom goes wrong with extra length. A too-short ski means less stability on the snow. Touring skis are narrower than regular skis; that's why people call them "skinny skis." The wooden ones come with either lighastone or steel edges.

Fortunately, bindings for your XC skis are also inexpensive. In fact, a cross-country skier pays less than one-fourth of what it costs to buy the complex, heavy release bindings of regular skis. XC bindings are simple enough, consisting of only a few parts which guarantee you complete freedom at the heel. In other words, you can move the back of your foot up and down while you ski.

Poles are equally basic; they should reach up to the height of your armpits, as short poles involve more hard work when climbing, especially on steep slopes. The material can be bamboo or metal.

Boots? Forget about those extra high, extra heavy downhill boots that the lift skiers wear. For cross-country excursions, the special boot is advisable. They're lightweight and comfortable. The most expensive touring boots cost about one-fourth the price of regular ski boots. Some youngsters actually start skiing in work shoes or hiking boots. (Certain bindings will work for either.)

The best part of cross-country skiing is that any warm clothes will do. Unlike the usual resort fashion wear—elegant parkas, nifty, stylish sweaters, or expensive shirts—*any warm garments* suffice for the beginning cross-country skier. There is no point in spending money at a specialty shop; your regular winter wear will do in most instances.

A young man or woman can tour in any warm clothes that keep out the snow. Think in layers. Long woolen underwear, a turtleneck, a flannel shirt, an old sweater, one pair each of

A cross-country skier goes slowly enough to appreciate the beautiful Canadian landscape. *(Canadian Tourist Office)*

light and heavy socks, lined mittens or waterproof gloves, a warm cap that fits over your ears, and a long loose jacket or an old windbreaker make up the outfit of the basic cross-country skier.

What about ski pants? Remember that you need some freedom of motion. A pair of knickers with long socks is fine. Or a wide, sturdy pair of corduroy pants. Some young skiers wear their jeans, gym suits, or sweat suits. This is okay, too, especially on a golf course. In the mountains, though, the weather can change fast, and better clothing–a goose down jacket, for instance–comes in handy.

Always take a pack along so that you can peel off some layers if you get too warm. All in all, cross-country (or "Nordic") skiers are a special breed to whom fancy fashion is not important.

THE BASIC EASY-TO-LEARN TECHNIQUE

"If you can walk, you can cross-country ski," goes one slogan. Want to get started? Pick a flat area. Ask an older experienced brother or sister to come, then watch the XC skier's smooth glide across the snow.

It's time to try gliding yourself without poles. Keep your knees bent. ("Like an Indian sneaking through the grass," instructors say.) Your rear foot kicks; your forward foot slides. Now reverse the process.

It isn't much more difficult *with* ski poles. Swing one arm forward and upward, then your other. Kick and glide! Your knees must remain well-bent. The secret is always the rhythmic sliding motion. The stronger the kick, the longer the gliding phase.

Actually, with the proper ski wax, you can even glide uphill. (You can also use a "herringbone" climb in steeper terrain.)

On slight downgrades, you can use both poles at the same time. This is called "double poling." But unlike regular skiing, where you thrust the poles behind your bindings, the cross-country ski action takes place near the ski tips.

You'll marvel at the graceful sight of a long-time cross-country skier, especially the racer. One coach suggests that you study the flawless motions. Watch how he drives his knee forward in an effort to stretch out a couple more inches from his glide. Pay attention to his kick, how perfectly timed it is to gain the maximum thrust forward. Notice how his hand releases the pole, holding it with thumb and forefinger only, as the poling stroke is complete, and how his wrist snaps backwards for additional thrust and for a split second of rest to his arm. Eventually, you'll pick up other XC techniques. For instance, you'll make yourself lean forward on the downhill stretches, so that you don't fall. You'll learn how to stand up again after a fall. (Bring your feet close to the body and use the poles as a platform to get up.) The "wedge" will help you slow down on downhill portions. And, when standing, a complete change of direction can be made by means of the "kick turn." For turning, you can often employ a skating step, with the weight on the skated ski. There are, of course, many refinements to the turns.

Many young people learn these and other skills from their elders in one or two outings. Some enlist in cross-country ski schools available at ski areas, resorts, lodges, and inns. Still others take lessons that are available from various recreation departments (including the YMCA and YWCA).

Proper ski waxing always helps. To be sure, it is best to wax at room temperatures before you go out into the cold. Don't wait until you hit the trail. Let the waxed skis stand outside for a while before placing them in the snow. Otherwise, the flakes will stick to the bottoms. Proper waxing is essential, even if you ski in a city park. It becomes even more important if you glide up or down in hilly country. A steep trail can only be managed with correctly prepared skis. If yours are new wooden models, ask a ski shop to sell you some pine tar and two waxes. Remember these simple rules: 1. Use softer wax for softer and warmer snow. 2. The harder and colder the snow, the harder the wax. Fortunately, the same standard products are good for downhill as well as uphill.

As you graduate to more expensive skis, you may consider models with prewaxed surfaces. Some consist of plastics or "fishscale" patterns. A cloth base is also popular. It allows you to ski down as well as up a mountain. One of the pioneers of synthetic XC skis is F. Kneissl, an Austrian, whose products are popular in the U.S.

WHERE TO GO

A beginner's first outing should be limited to some easy terrain, a golf course or a large, fairly flat city park. (A few inches of snow on grass are enough.) If you live in the country, you can assemble some friends or older siblings and perhaps cross the fields, skiing from one farm to the next.

Later, it might be a good idea to pick some sort of desti-

Cross-country skiing can be done on flat land or on gentle meadows. *(Chris Rud photo, Winter Park, CO)*

nation. Do you know an easy route that leads to an old cabin? Do you remember a snow-buried road that climbs to a fire tower? Or a spot from where you had a good view while hiking last summer? Do you recall an abandoned little ghost town you first saw on horseback?

Go there with some experienced companions.

The wonderful advantage of the cross-country scene is that you seldom need to ask your parents for help. You don't have to travel far in winter. (By contrast, unless you live in Vermont or Colorado, you may be some distance away from the big ski resorts.) Most big ski complexes nowadays also provide cross-country trails for the public. Many of these trails are well marked.

Some resorts post maps at intersections on trees. You'll also be told by the area XC rental shop about the quality of each trail. You'll learn if it's for beginners, intermediates, or experts. The super XC skiers demand the steepest, most rugged runs, as well as the longest.

It's not wise to test your mettle against expert terrain if you've only skied once or twice. Nor would it be smart to explore a ski area cross-country setup on your own. Go with friends or with your parents.

How are various ski tours rated by the people who organize them? One typical mountain club with a large touring program defines the various kinds of trips like this:

> Easy–generally under 5 miles with not more than 1,000 feet of elevation gain. Emphasis on relaxed pace for all levels.
>
> Moderate–generally 5–10 miles with not more than 2,000 feet of elevation gain. Emphasis on mildly strenuous pace. Beginners should be able to handle easy trips well in all snow conditions before attempting a moderate trip.
>
> Advanced–emphasis on a difficult tour while realizing a planned objective. Check with leader.
>
> Overnight–night will be spent at cabins or shelters. Sleeping bag and other special equipment required. Participants must be able to ski with a backpack and be prepared to carry their share

of group food and cooking equipment. Overnight trips are for experienced XC skiers, and you need to be part of a large group. The club takes care of all the transportation arrangements. (See the addresses of mountain clubs and ski clubs in other chapters.)

If you live in mountain country, your high school may offer some XC outings. Certain churches form groups of young touring skiers. The regional offices of the U.S. Ski Association also go in for cross-country skiing. The USSA devised a worthwhile "Ski Tourer's Pledge."

> I will protect the land and natural resources of the land on which I ski. I will make it my personal business to leave the land in such a condition that except for the tracks of my skis upon the snow no one will ever know that I was there. I will always treat the land gently so that I may return in the future and be welcomed as an old friend.

XC PROGRAMS AND DESTINATIONS: SOME USEFUL IDEAS

Study a North American map. For a moment, forget about the Rockies as they sweep south from Alaska to Mexico for some 3,300 miles. If you live in Colorado, Utah, Idaho, in Alberta or British Columbia, in New Mexico or Montana, you already know about the nearest XC territory. Young people from New England's White Mountains and Green Mountains are aware of the many possibilities in their neck of the woods. To be sure, topnotch ski resorts such as New Hampshire's Waterville Valley or Stowe, Vermont, have a lot of experience in trail planning. Easterners will also flock to the excellent trail network in the Adirondacks. On the outskirts of New York City, Ward Pound Ridge Reservation features 4,500 acres of beautiful woodland trails and the Palisades with 6 miles of novice trails. A few hours to the north are the Catskills and a little further the Shawangunk Mountains, with the vast trail systems of Lake Minnewaska and Lake Mohonk. Philadelphians are not far from the Black Forest

Trails and the Pocono Mountains. New Jersey communities are close to the picturesque Stokes Forest. Think of the Berkshires and the Taconic Range of Massachusetts or Quebec's well-developed Laurentians.

There are Maryland's Catoctin Mountain National Park touring trails near Washington, D.C., and further south near Richwood, West Virginia, the Monongahela National Forest with miles of unplowed roads. Further south, the 5,000 acres within the 154,000 acres of the Mt. Rogers National Park near Marion, Virginia, are popular with tourers. The southern states offer touring in the Blue Ridge Parkway and Pisgah National Forest and the Mt. Mitchell State Park, with the highest elevation in the East.

Ohio's five state parks are well suited for ski touring. In fact, large cities like Cleveland connect with easy-to-reach cross-country terrain.

The Midwest and South offer more hilly touring terrain than most people suppose. Consider Michigan's Muskegon State Park with its trails that lead to crests overlooking Lake Michigan. A more experienced young skier might try the rugged Rock Pile Mountain Trail in the Clark National Forest of Missouri.

The Canadian flatlands, extending from Hudson's Bay west to the Rockies, have hundreds of trails. The Cypress Hills Provincial Park in Saskatchewan, for example, is characterized by high bluffs and deep valleys.

The South has many ranges and chains that are good cross-country bets. The Blue Ridge Mountains of North Carolina, to name one chain, invite touring. Another high-country area of the South is the Great Smoky Mountains National Park in Tennessee. (Remember that even a little snow goes a long way for XC.) More ski touring areas in the South—the Ozark Mountains of northern Arkansas and southern Missouri, the Cohutta Mountains of northern Georgia, and the national forests of the southern Appalachians.

Move west, where the Colorado Rockies are full of possibilities. Choose among 54 peaks of over 14,000 feet and 1,100 that exceed 10,000 feet. Ski the well-marked trails of Idlewild, at Hideaway Park, Colorado, or Copper Mountain or Keystone. And so to New Mexico and its high country, and to the less-visited elevations in parts of Idaho and Montana. One can cross-country ski into Idaho's wrinkled Sawtooths; there are lots of remote trails with Alpine scenery. (Consider the Lost River Range.)

The Rockies are paralleled by the Alaskan-Canadian Coast Mountains, the Cascades, and the Sierra Nevada. Cross-country skiing is almost everywhere. For more information about touring trails, write to the Ski Touring Council, Troy, VT 05868, or S.T.C., 5101 39th Avenue, Long Island City, NY 11104. In Canada, write, Department of Tourism, Fish and Game, 150 est, Boulevard Saint-Cyrille, Quebec, Canada.

A FEW PRECAUTIONS

The pleasant thing about cross-country skiing is that you're free. You can go almost anywhere. Use the established trails or create your own route. Cross-country skiing requires only a few inches of snow, so you can ski even in the early spring. You can go slow or fast, near or far.

There are certain dangers, however. Smart young tourers listen to the weather reports before setting out. It doesn't pay to take chances with extra-cold temperatures, winds, a possible blizzard. As you ski, the windchill factor will increase the brutal cold. Even for short tours into the wilderness, a small pack is necessary. A two-hour outing? Take along a few candy bars, some nuts, perhaps some extra clothes, a compass, and a trail map. It is better to dress more warmly than you have to; you can always take off some things.

Before starting out, tell someone that you're going. And where. And for how long. Never travel alone. A party of four is best.

Some young skiers in New England come to harm each

These young people took cross-country skiing one step further. They're racing! *(U.S. Ski Association)*

winter because of overconfidence. They ski too fast and then exhaust themselves. Or they go too far, forgetting all about distances. They take risks by leaving the packed, marked cross-country trails and venturing without a compass, maps, or knowledge into uncharted, rough country. If they're unlucky, the tourers may get lost. If they get exhausted in cold weather, they may lose heat fast and risk hypothermia. Hypothermia means subnormal body temperatures and can lead to a complete physical collapse. (For more information about this topic, read Chapter 12.)

That's why an experienced leader or a professional touring guide becomes so important on longer wilderness trips. In the West, you need to take an additional precaution. There may be avalanches, those roaring, thundering, killing snow slides. Warning signs are usually posted at ski areas, in national parks, or in much-traveled national forests. Obey the signs. But how about the higher touring country? How about the slide-prone mountains of Utah, Colorado, Idaho, California, Wyoming?

Avalanche danger can be avoided by asking someone who should know. Contact a Forest or National Park Ranger. Inquire at the nearest specialty ski shop. Take the person's advice.

In the high western mountains, steep slopes may slide. The demolished, cut trees tell about the paths of previous avalanches. There is increased danger under (and on) these steep slopes after heavy snows, followed by windstorms or a rapid rise of temperature. Stay out of avalanche country if you want to continue touring.

CROSS-COUNTRY RACING FOR YOUNG PEOPLE

Some young cross-country skiers eventually want to compete. Ask your local newspaper's sports department about Citizens' Races. Every winter, dozens of these take place in the eastern and western ski states, as well as in Michigan and Wisconsin. (There is even such a yearly race outside Cleveland, Ohio.)

Anybody can race. Age is of little importance because you can register in your own group. There is usually a ten-and-under class, as well as ages twelve-and-under. Teenager's times are judged against those of their own peers, just as grownups compete only in their own age groups.

Boys and girls of various ages generally race against each other.

All in all, there may be two hundred to five hundred people of all sizes and skills. But your time is measured only against those in your group.

Distances vary. Some races are only three kilometers, which means a much faster pace than the longer races. Some citizens' competitions go on for 8 kilometers. A 10-km event is frequent, and there are some 13-km or 15-km races. Try to go slowly enough to enjoy it and to make it to the finish line.

This isn't as hard as you may think. "Kids are tougher per pound than adults," says Bob Tucker, a long-time American cross-country official, whose own nine and ten-year-old boys enjoy competitions. Tucker says that preteeners don't need to train much if they lead an active life and do other sports. Teenagers or grownups should put in at least five to six hours a week, however. They need to build up endurance. Their hearts and lungs need to get used to the exertion. For some, it may pay off later with college racing.

If they start young enough, some kids may even make it into the Olympic XC team. Take one U.S. Olympian named Billy Koch, for instance. This young Vermonter is not easy to forget because he won a silver medal for a 30-km race at the 1976 winter Olympics. His coach still remembers the boy at the age of twelve. "Billy had stars in his eyes! He skied every Sunday afternoon with the college kids of Putney, Vermont. They went long distances. Billy had trouble keeping up. But he trained! How he trained!" Like all motivated XC competitors, Billy ran hard all summer. He hiked and climbed. He skied hundreds of miles each winter week, which isn't unusual for top Nordic racers.

You don't have to race. In fact, most young people never try it. They cross-country ski for other reasons. They want to get out into the fresh air and be part of Mother Nature.

Scandinavians, because they toured for thousands of years, always appreciate these quiet pleasures. One Swedish father sums it up well for North Americans. "The sport is not an end in itself," he says, "but a means of enjoying the meadows and forests. Of coming close to the great white, mysterious wilderness. Yes, touring is a good winter sport for the mountains."

In the next chapter, we'll examine a completely different type of skiing.

CHAPTER 7

Alpine Skiing

SOME GOOD REASONS

Coming down a snowy hill on skis can be the purest of joys. You feel light and detached. You move with a dance-like, easy rhythm. Your arms are like wings and stabilizers, and the turns seem to take care of themselves. At times, you seem to float. At other times, you feel the onrush of great speed. Skiing can be the most enjoyable, most exciting, and most relaxing of sports.

There is only the blue sky, the well-scrubbed trees, the upholstered peak, and you. The air quickens your breathing. You see no smog; at the heights, dust doesn't exist. You hear no screeching cars, no sirens, no slamming doors. There is only silence. Many young people need this quiet, especially if they live in a large city. The clean world stays with you for days.

Ski areas make a pretty picture. The shimmering, rolling terrain, the possibility of higher mountains, the snow-bordered fir branches—all have a good effect on you. The colors seem lively. You see the skiers on the chair lift; the underside of their fiberglass skis are stark yellow or green, even bright red. The black skis contrast with the morning sky. Some ski clothes dazzle the eyes. The parkas have cheery patterns. The faces shine. Somehow, everyone seems to look handsome here.

Skiing the Canadian Rockies means massive scenery. *(British Columbia Government Photograph)*

Why take up skiing? If you're a skier now, you already know the freedom of darting, leaping, gliding, and weaving downward through a white world. You know that skiing can be a lark, an exploration, a search for beauty, total flight, action, a moment of truth, a battle with the elements, total quiet, privacy, a ballet dance, a sunbath, and always a health giver. Teenagers excel at it after a few lessons.

Once you can ski, the mountain is all yours.

You often get the feeling of exploration, especially in the Rocky Mountains. You only have to leave the packed Utah runs and go off—but not alone—to one of the unexplored expanses. The shoulders of the peaks can be swimming in the purest sunlight. Or you can pick a cold day. The brooding clouds will open, and the thick flakes muffle all sounds. You no longer hear the skiers on nearby trails. You pull out the hood and fasten the yellow goggles before your eyes. You're Byrd exploring the Antarctic! You're Peary at the North Pole!

ONE, TWO, THREE: GET READY FOR SKIING!

Skiing takes some preparation. Remember that if you go in for summer activities like horseback riding, tennis, or hiking, you'll have an easier time in winter. You'll enjoy the sport more if you're not totally out of shape. And you'll be less tired afterward. Jogging or running in summer helps you get ready for winter. Jogging loosens you, strengthens muscles, develops your wind, increases your stamina. It's natural for a boy to run hard. A girl shouldn't feel self-conscious about running. She can do so in a YWCA or in a park. If she wants to, she can have a friend along.

Other young skiers do a lot of waterskiing. Or they go in for the kind of fishing that requires walking upstream. Or they play earnest golf without the benefit of those electrical carts. Or they're hockey players, basketball players, skate boarders, surfers. You'll be *safer* on skis if you do a few simple exercises in late autumn. Get into condition before the first snow falls. Here are the traditional preseason exercises.

- Walk, in flat-heeled shoes, because ski boots are flat. Walk at least five or six blocks every day. Walk up and down stairs. For preski purposes, do it backwards. (Just be sure that you have your foot firmly planted on the right step.)
- Try the "bus rider's special." Balance evenly on both feet; lean forward, rise on toes, bounce (so you feel loose all over), then lower the heels to the floor.
- Knee bends are familiar to most people. For skiing, the half bend is better than the deep knee bend. Don't squat clear down to your heels. Stop as though sitting on an 18-inch stool.

OFF TO SKI SCHOOL

Skiing takes practice. Could you pick up the basics on your own? Some teens are talented; they just watch good skiers and copy them. On occasion, one of your parents may be an

You must get into shape for skiing at a gym or outdoors. *(Bob Krueger, Aspen)*

able teacher. Most people, though, prefer to join a class. This is a sociable thing to do and you learn a great deal, even in a single morning.

Classes usually meet at 10 A.M. The ski school bell rings. The meeting place is well marked. Instructors are chosen for their patience, and they're trained to detect (and correct) your skiing errors. Even the smallest North American ski areas now have a ski school. Start with a half-day lesson and use the afternoon for practice. Lessons are essential on your first day, which also happens to be the hardest. Your second day will be much easier.

A few young people are fortunate; they live in places like Stowe, Vermont, or Aspen, Colorado, where they learn to ski as part of their school sports program.

If you reside in a large city, ask your parents to enroll you in a special ski club for young people. Here you get bused to the nearest slope plus ski lessons. Expenses are generally low because you return home in the evening. Churches, YMCAs, ski lift companies, and even department stores run such programs.

Some ski schools, like one sponsored by a store in Minneapolis, Minnesota, have been outstandingly successful. In San Francisco, a club always fetches an enrollment of about 1,500 boys and girls. How do you find the right club? Just visit the closest ski specialty shop. Here you can usually get information. Even midwestern states like Nebraska or Kansas now go in for junior skiing; the clubs usually take you to the slopes for a weekend. This is ideal if your parents don't ski.

Some families travel to ski areas or resorts where one can take lessons.

What happens in ski school? What will you be doing? For a starter, you'll have to learn how to carry your skis to the meeting place. It's important to carry equipment correctly because: 1) the skis could hit someone, or 2) the equipment can slip out of your grasp and be damaged.

Your gear doesn't belong under the arms. Instead, skis go

on your shoulders, tips forward. The bindings face out; otherwise, they'll cut into your shoulders. For better balance, center the skis. To lighten the load for a longer walk, you slide the poles under the skis.

At the meeting place, the instructor will familiarize you with the workings of your ski poles; if you need to, you'll also get some immediate help with your ski bindings.

SKI TECHNIQUE

Many ski schools favor the "Graduated Length Method," or GLM. Short skis are much easier to handle. Thanks to this invention, timid beginners become lift-riding skiers often within one hour. A morning class of first-timers can make and turn down a mountain's more gentle slopes by lunchtime. The teacher may encourage you to try a little walking on the level ground. That's how you get the feel of your gear. You'll find that walking on skis is not much more difficult than walking without them. The trick is to slide and to take small steps. Push yourself alternately with the right and left ski pole. While you're on level ground, remember *not* to lift your skis. Sliding takes less effort.

How about a little uphill hike? The easiest way to climb is by "sidestepping." Instructors like to compare this to walking up a set of stairs *sideways*. The maneuver is simple enough. Plant your ski poles for support, lift your uppermost ski above the ground, and put it down a foot higher up the mountain. Now let the lower ski follow until your two skis are together again. You can only climb this way if you're horizontal to the slope. Take small steps. Another tip: Whether in motion or resting, your skis must be parallel at all times. Don't get them crossed.

You'll next be taught the *schuss*, or a short downhill run. It is easy if you lean forward. Your slope will be a gentle one.

If you're a beginning skier, the *wedge* becomes most useful; it allows you to slow down and to stop. The teacher may com-

This Winter Park, Colorado, skier shows what the sport is all about . . . pure joy! *(Chris Rud, Winter Park, CO)*

pare it to a slice (or wedge) of cake. The tips of your skis are together; the tails apart at equal angles. Your body weight is evenly distributed. This helps you to "plow" the snow, that is, to brake. Try it on an easy slope first. Push off, then bring the ski tips together. You'll quickly notice the braking effect. Especially when you employ the inside ski edges, with the tails of your skis far apart.

In time, you'll learn to control your descent with a more interesting and efficient method.

The wedge exercises teach you that with equal weight distribution the skis will move in a straight line.

Now what happens if *one* ski is more heavily weighted? You'll find that it will then turn. Or to put it another way: weight transfer becomes the novice's turning force.

Instructors will also show you the traverse, which means downhill skiing *across* the slope. Actually, you'll find traversing as easy as going down straight. The secret weapon: your ski edges. (The edges are the long metal strips under your skis; the employment of the edges is called "edging.")

When you cross the slope the first time, the ski facing the valley is sometimes called the downhill ski. The other ski, higher on the mountain, is the uphill ski. Put your weight at all times on the *downhill* ski. You simply keep your upper body over it. This gentle body-angling weights the downhill ski. The uphill ski and your hip are slightly advanced. When you master a traverse, you can manage practically any slope.

Most ski schools will soon graduate you to "side-slipping" during a traverse. You merely release your edges, which allows you to slide down the mountain. The use of your knees and the proper body position will help you control the travel. The side-slip is good preparation for the various turns. Some schools prefer to let you do wedge turns, then stem turns, and finally parallel turns.

One last word about technique. Skiing used to be an effort-demanding sport. This has changed with the modern ski systems. Skiing has now become smooth, simple, easygoing, economical. The jerky style of the old days has given way to fluid, continuous motions. Your position should be as natural as possible. You don't have to lean out at an extreme angle. Experts also agree that the modern ski systems make few

Skier inscribes tracks into new snow. *(Wyoming State)*

demands on the muscles. You only need balance. Gravity and proper positions will do the rest.

The good skier can make his turn as long or short as he chooses; the expert can let a cornice lift him through the air, then stop almost on a dime. Gravity does the rest. The mountain pulls, increasing your speed. The chair lift towers become a reddish blur. Controlled speed is a joy; this is why many skiers ski.

EQUIPMENT POINTERS FOR YOUNG PEOPLE

How often will you ski? Just for one week a year? At different places each season? These questions are important when it comes to equipment. The young, once-a-year skier does best by renting. You need not rent at your hometown ski shop; instead, you'll travel lighter by doing business with an area ski shop.

If you will be skiing often, consider at first renting instead of buying your skis. Any ski shop will lend you the equipment for a few dollars a day, by the day. This includes boots, skis, and poles. This helps you get familiar with various brands.

After three or four times on the slopes you'll want to acquire a pair of skis. There are two theories about buying skis. Some people start with the most inexpensive skis and then move up to more costly fiberglass. Other people begin with the best brandname models, which last a long time and ski with a winged, inspiring ease. A compromise often works best: Buy a lesser-known brand of fiberglass skis. These are almost as good as the famous ones, obeying when you order them to steer left and forgiving mistakes. Young people do well by buying larger sizes because they'll outgrow them.

Instructors agree that the same premise applies to ski boots. Someone who is still growing doesn't need fancy boots and would be foolish to spend \$150 to \$200 for new plastic wonder models. Ski boots must fit well, and only expert personnel can help there. Unless you get a perfect fit, you'll be uncom-

Youngsters learn to jump at various ski areas. *(Winter Park, CO)*

The popularity of skiing is shown in this photo. The youngsters are signed up by a Denver department store for the ski trip. *(Loveland Basin, CO)*

fortable, won't be able to handle your skis properly, and will be more likely to tumble. Boots should be snug, but not tight, and there cannot be pressure anywhere.

Remember that boots translate a skier's motion to the ski; boots help turning and stopping in the snow. A well-fitting boot will prevent accidents since a skier's feet control the edges. A speeding skier can fall as a result of poorly fitting boots. Don't let a salesperson bamboozle you into buying the first pair you are trying on. A clerk's impatience is a sure sign of an inferior store; no good shop will be in a hurry to get rid of unsuitable merchandise.

Apart from boots, ski bindings may be your most important item. That's where a truly experienced specialty shop can really help the serious skier.

There are some bindings that require the knowledge of an engineer and the contortion ability of a Yogi. These are not for the average skier. More parts can freeze and go haywire. A binding should be easy to get into. Various makes of bindings are available, especially designed for a youngster's smaller weight. Two of the best ones–Salomon and Look–Nevada–are imported from France.

It pays to put some money into a binding. For one thing, it may save you a broken leg. And a good binding lasts; you can mount it on your next pair of skis.

The salesperson should be able to explain the mechanism. He should teach how to get in and out of the binding and tell you how it releases. *Listen carefully to these explanations.* Find out how to adjust the mechanism. Adjustment systems vary. For some bindings, fingers can be used. For others, a coin or a screwdriver are the needed tools. Ask the area ski shop to check it.

Today poles are lightweight. The proper length of the pole is found by standing upright and bending the forearm at a right angle in front of your body. The grip of the pole should then rest comfortably in the palm of your hand. This rule applies to young people as well.

You will also need ski gloves or mittens when skiing. If the gloves you've bought don't keep you warm, you probably selected too tight a fit, which restricts finger movement and crushes insulating air space. Try inner liners for added warmth. For really cold weather, mittens are generally warmer.

Goggles are essential in a blizzard; you'll need sunglasses for good weather at high altitudes.

IF YOU'RE DISABLED

Every February, you can watch a rather unique ski race at Winter Park, Colorado. Through the gates at intervals of three minutes descend a number of skiers. They're clocked at an average of 40 mph. Unusual? Not for the ordinary ski racer. But these young people are not ordinary. Some of them have only one leg; others have only one arm. A few ski without hands. The rest fly down the mountain despite paralyzed

Disabled skier skis races, too. *(Lloyd Coleman, Winter Park, CO)*

The joys of stirring up powder snow! *(Colorado Ski Country USA)*

joints, missing kneecaps, absent toes, or stiffened backs. They're all disabled skiers of various ages. Although amputees, they're all winners.

Skiing requires coordination and balance. The loss of an arm will change performance. With only one ski pole, the skier will have trouble making his turns or trying to get up a hill. Practice and determination will make a one-armed skier as good as a two-armed one.

The sudden loss of a leg is much more serious, yet thanks to "outrigger" (or crutch) skis any amputee can learn to ski.

You'll see young amputee skiers in many parts of the country. You'll also see boys like Steve, who has multiple sclerosis. Steve came to Colorado with his parents on vacation. He had never walked without the aid of crutches. Ed, his instructor, began by supporting Steve between his knees, and they skied down the hill. Next, Ed and his wife held a broomstick horizontally, and Steve skied holding on to the handle. He loved it, and his enthusiasm grew. By the end of the week, Steve

Exuberance on skis. *(Colorado Ski Country USA)*

skied with Ed following him, holding only a rope tied to Steve's waist for balance. Upon Steve's return home, he soon walked without his crutches. His parents credit much of the progress to the confidence gained through skiing.

A pole or stick is also used for blind skiers. Others receive help from an instructor ringing a bell at each dip in the mountain.

If you're disabled, give skiing a chance.

SKIING ON A LOW ALLOWANCE

Ski equipment is expensive, and if yours is an average family, you'll try to shave costs. Can it be done? Just ask the "ski bum" who spends entire winters on skis. Expense-paring systems can be adopted by everyone.

First of all, whether you are a boy or girl, there is a chance to save on ski clothes. You need to be warm, not up-to-date. Unless you go to a fashionable resort, you should forget about fashion. Last year's parka, available at a discount store or at a big sporting goods store, will work just as well. An old-model ski pant is acceptable, too. Jeans or farmer's overalls are popular. A sweater need not be bought in an exclusive ski specialty shop; Montgomery Ward and Sears Roebuck do just fine.

You find that your allowance goes further by buying very early (October–November) or very late (March–April). Around Christmas, stores demand the highest prices. Ask your parents and take advantage of end-of-the-season clearance sales. If you need skis *now,* keep in mind that last year's model may be available at a discount of 25 percent to 50 percent and worth every penny saved. Consider ski swaps arranged by clubs, churches, or the ski patrol; study your hometown paper for classified ads.

There's another good angle for novice skiers. They can acquire whole outfits at special prices. Most shops now advertise skis, bindings, boots, and poles at one total package price. Some money can also be saved by looking for used skis and used poles. To know if the used stuff is worth the money stick to a specialty ski shop.

"SKI BUMMING"

Last winter a young girl was skiing down a Colorado hill. It had snowed the night before, and she was cutting a swath through the bright white snow. She couldn't have been more than twelve years old. She was already a fairly good skier, even in deep snow. You could see her blonde pigtails bobbing. As she zoomed past the other skiers, she let out a wild yodel. She wasn't showing off. She was only showing she was having the time of her life.

It turned out the girl was a ski bum. She got a free lift ticket by working for three hours at the base lodge. Her job was picking up empty trays and dishes.

Some young people earn lift tickets by helping to pack the slopes. They don't have to be very good skiers for that work, and it's excellent exercise besides. There are other part-time

These youngsters are actually skiing in Arizona. *(Tucson Visitors Bureau)*

jobs available. You can find out about them by talking to the area manager.

Not all young people want to work or find jobs. But they take other shortcuts. Many skiers pool their car rides to the areas, for example. If you assemble five other guys or gals for a 50-mile ride, the expenses will be low. Lots of skiers bring their own sandwiches, so they cut the cost of expensive area cafeterias. Regard ski touring (see Chapter 6) as a possibility. It saves you the cost of ski lifts and can be quite safe in the company of others. A ski tour provides a means of getting away from the crowds and enjoying the solitude and beauty of the mountains and countryside.

WHY YOUR FOLKS DON'T NEED TO TAKE YOU TO A BIG RESORT

If you're a new skier, a small hill will do fine. Forget all about the fancy tramway or "gondola" lifts of the big resorts. To ski there costs you much more than at a tiny hill with a simple T-bar lift.

Some families use their winter vacations for skiing. Others spend a weekday on the slopes. They are the lucky ones. They live in the mountainous regions of the West or New England.

Other people prefer to ski on weekends in one of the nation's 1,200 areas. An Arizona family can reach the ski center of Santa Fe, New Mexico, in half a day's drive. The White Mountains of New Hampshire are only a few hours from Boston, Massachusetts. Some enthusiastic New York State skiers tackle Canada's Laurentians over a weekend. Families are skiing in the Ozarks, the Great Smoky Mountains, the Catskills, the Adirondacks. There is even skiing in the South—at Gatlinburg, Tennessee.

In the East and Midwest, the hills are more timbered. The trails are shorter and the country is flatter than in the West. With modern snow-making equipment, the ski seasons

Ski club season ends with costume party. *(William Schmid, Loveland Basin, CO)*

there are not much shorter. On the other hand, Montana, Colorado, and Oregon have mountains with year-round snow.

SKIING SAFELY: HOW TO AVOID THE FIRST AID STATION

Skiing isn't as dangerous as it sounds; only two or three in a thousand skiers wind up on a rescue toboggan, and not necessarily with a fracture. (Sprains are more frequent.)

By sticking to good equipment, using common sense on the slopes, and doing preseason exercise, you can prevent accidents on the slopes.

Untrained muscles just won't cope with the strain of skiing. Without conditioning, the skier may get hurt on the slopes. The result can be a fracture. Weak ligaments can snap; a tense joint can be injured by a sprain in no time. In fact, physical tension is the fate of the untrained skier. The under-exercised skier is in danger.

Don't ski when you're tired or famished. Avoid skiing beyond your ability. You must always be able to stop. Don't act like a downhill racer until you are one. The surveys indicate that the season's first days are the most dangerous. After that, the injuries come chiefly to those who ski out of control. You must adapt your skill to the terrain. Just as an inexperienced mountain climber doesn't begin with a 90-degree rock face, so the new skier must first learn to handle the easy trails. Avoid extrasteep runs until you can ski them.

It is best, of course, to know the mountain layout. If the area is new to you, the study of a free trail map pays dividends. It helps you to choose runs that you're capable of handling. The map also gives you a bearing to find the various lifts. North American ski areas help you with the use of trail mark-

This is called free style skiing. The trick is easy to learn for young people who are in good physical condition *(Chris Rud, Winter Park, CO)*

ers. These indicate the grade of difficulty. Several colors and shapes, beginning with a green square, show the ease or toughness of a ski descent.

Accidents can be reduced by keeping away from ski lifts until you're ready. Missing ski edges, warped skis, or loose boots cause mishaps. Pay attention to your ski bindings. Have them properly adjusted by the best ski shop in town or at the ski area.

Dull edges will brake less effectively. Although you can sharpen the edges with the assistance of a file, at least once during the skiing season this should be done expertly by your specialized sporting goods dealer. Skis should be stored singly, without tying them together, in a dry space.

It also makes sense to dress properly for skiing in cold temperatures. Wear long johns and a turtleneck, in addition to shirt and sweater. If the temperatures are below zero, the half-hour chair lift ride can chill you to the bone. Thaw out at the summit warming house first. Or do some kneebends on your skis. Limber up on an easy slope.

Know the rules of the ski road. The pistes, or ski runs, demand the same courtesy as our superhighways.

Ski areas and the U.S. Ski Association, along with the National Ski Patrol, created a "Skier's Code."

The Skier's Code

1. Ski under control.
2. When skiing downhill and overtaking another skier, avoid the skier below.
3. When meeting another skier in traversing the slope, pass to the right.
4. Do not stop where you will obstruct a trail or the loading or unloading area of lift, and do not stop where you cannot be seen from above.
5. When entering a trail or slope from a side or intersecting trail, check for approaching downhill skiers.
6. When standing, check for approaching downhill skiers before resuming your run.

7. When walking or climbing in a ski area, wear skis and keep to the side of the trail or slope.
8. Wear safety straps or other devices to prevent runaway skis.
9. Keep off closed trails and posted areas.

Three useful addresses for more information:

National Ski Areas Association
61 South Main St.
West Hartford, CT 06107

United States Ski Association
1463 Larimer Square
Denver, CO 80202

Ski Industries America
P.O. Box 2270
Peabody, MA 01960

CHAPTER 8

Ski Racing

WHO SHOULD RACE?

This is a book about mountain sports, not competitive sports. Not many young people from most of North America's middle or southern section have an opportunity to become racers.

All the same, you may live in mountainous regions. Or perhaps you have parents with enough patience and funds who are willing to take you to a ski area during many winter weekends. A few words about ski competition may, therefore, be in order.

Who should race? And what sort of personal traits does it take? First of all, bear in mind that you must be able to stand speed.

Alpine ski racing consists of slalom, where you do well with technique and skill; giant slalom, which means a somewhat faster pace; and downhill, which is almost entirely speed and stamina.

Both girls and boys should be able to handle all three types of competitions. Often, you have no choice but to run downhills along with the much shorter slaloms.

To run a downhill, you must learn and enjoy and handle speed. It is not difficult for those who train. Remember that skiing at 50 and 60 mph cannot be done at once; you build up to it slowly, over several seasons.

Training demands some self-discipline from a young person. It takes a lot to go through the exhausting preseason fitness session. You'll need to accept the unpleasant parts of ski racing (like the sometimes tedious reruns of a slalom course) along with the excitement and fun.

Self-discipline should be coupled with pride. One cannot become much of an athlete without personal pride in doing the best possible work, both on the ski slope and in school. Pride in constantly seeking perfection of technique. Pride in the equipment you have chosen, and even pride in your appearance.

A coach once said that a racer can only succeed if he or she has a positive attitude. The big-name racers know this, and they've learned to believe in themselves and to reject failure. They'd never let a lost race bother them. But the beginners—and sometimes the young—do not always realize this power of positive thinking. It helps to overcome the actual stress of the race itself.

Young Canadian racers line up for a group shot on Alberta slopes. *(Banff Tourist Department, Canada)*

You also require sportsmanship as a novice. What if you lose? Can you take it? You'll have to.

Dedication is important, too. This can involve some sacrifice and effort. A true champion must be able to give up the more pleasant aspects of life (like parties, for instance) to reach a final goal.

The competitive spirit fuels racing success.

You need personal health and you must maintain it. You can be well-conditioned, mentally ready, and even know you're going to win. But if you're not in good health, all of the hard work that goes into racing may be wasted.

WHERE AND HOW TO START

Where do you start? Should you perhaps begin with fun races? You've probably watched them at ski areas—contests where you crawl through barrels, or ski with an egg on a spoon, or run against elderly ladies and grandfathers. And why not?

Some people are lucky enough to ski in their school, as part of physical education. They start in elementary school races, if they're at that age level. You can also join a club and begin racing there.

Apart from scholastic and club skiing, there are hundreds of programs organized by ski areas (typical examples are Mammoth Mountain, Stowe, Vermont, and Loveland Basin, Colorado) and even by sports shops. Some other young people start in the (recreational) Nostar races held at many ski areas.

Summer racing schools always prove useful. Let's look at a typical one in Montana.

The Red Lodge International summer racing camp consumes only ten days per youngster. The first day provides a good clue to the rest: the young person rises in his carpeted dorm at 6:30, receives a massive breakfast, boards a bus, and then travels some 26 uphill miles to the eternal snows.

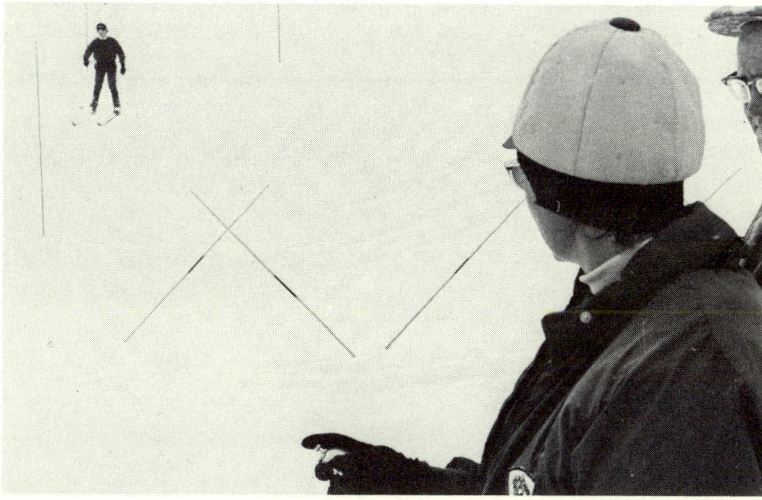

Youngest racers are already timed by volunteer official at Loveland Basin, Colorado. *(Curtis Casewit)*

Now comes the first chance to demonstrate skiing ability. While the ski coaches wait below, each camp customer zooms through a slalom course. The horde of 160 or so boys and girls (ages seven to eighteen) will then be split into seven groups, depending on the speed and form they just showed. Before the young skiers hit the steep glaciers they do some warmup "schussing" and swivelling. The instructors show consideration in case of bad weather; the groups watch ski movies or listen to lectures. In case of sunshine–and Montana summers are mostly pleasant–you streak through flags until mid-afternoon. Then it's time for the game rooms and pinball machines.

Such summer camps also concentrate on the art of taking care of equipment. At night, there are various lectures and visiting ski celebrities. The intense training has actually produced some of America's leading competitive talent. About 20 percent of the youngsters are girls, who sleep in their own special condominium and become strong by skiing with the boys. At Red Lodge, Kneissl, a leading ski maker, assists the junior racers with the maintenance.

In America, ski racing is supervised by the United States Ski Association and its divisions. It's the USSA that you should approach for all data regarding your racing. You'll find that there are slight variations in each USSA division in the grouping of competition. We call it classification. It all depends on your age and on your ability. At the age of fourteen, you move up the ladder through classification races. (See address listings.)

Don't worry about equipment at first. It's the boy or girl who counts, not the skis.

SOME DEFINITIONS OF VARIOUS RACES

Let's start with the most thrilling event, the downhill. A downhill race is usually 1½ to 3½ miles long, with sharp drop-offs, long runouts, sharp turns, and changes of terrain. There are about thirty control and direction gates. Girls have a shorter course and fewer gates. All racers must wear crash helmets.

Is downhill racing dangerous? More novices get hurt when doing a wedge turn than speeding downhill racers. The reason is fitness, fast reactions, training, and skill. Downhill is one event you either love or hate. Many young people find it exhilarating.

More than any other Alpine event, downhill is a state of mind. It's tough and demanding. The only way for a racer to become mentally prepared for it is to have experience on tough hills. Before you get on a downhill course you should be primed in the basics of the downhill turn, smooth-sensitive to the snow, and offensive as opposed to defense. ("If you don't attack the course, it will attack you," says one girl.) Get used to free skiing fast and loose over bumps. Try to ride and press on the back side of bumps rather than flying. Re-

A famous racer once said that children should only compete if they really want to. This girl obviously does! *(Curtis Casewit)*

member to research your line in a downhill by experimenting and watching others.

A slalom is held on a fairly short course with a good vertical drop. There are from fifty to seventy-five gates. If you are forced to ski through a gate, you are bound to improve your turning ability and your rhythm. You can keep the gates 12 to 15 feet apart and keep a distance of about 15 to 30 feet between gates.

The slalom combinations are now standard all over the world. These include "open gates," set horizontally to the slope; "closed gates," set vertically; "hairpins," which are two successive closed gates. Add one more vertically set gate, and you have a "flush"—a total of six flags along the fall line.

Recreational skiers should use only open gates.

Apart from being a great challenge, the gates and colored flags look very pretty against the white of the snow.

To become a slalom racer, you must be a flawless skier. Slalom also takes concentration and a great deal of skill, which only comes after many seasons of racing.

Your turn consists of three steps:

1) The approach
2) The main motion
3) The finish

Let's look at the various components, one by one. The approach begins with the poles held in front of you. Concentrate on balance. Watch the instructor as he keeps the lion's share of the weight on the downhill ski, then moves a pole to his downhill side at a 25-degree angle. He now leans his upper body downhill. Poling becomes important for the approach phase.

The poles set up your upper body for the main motion, the unweighting of the turn.

The giant slalom is faster than the slalom but not as fast as the downhill. A giant slalom requires a minimum of thirty gates including start and finish. The gates are at least 12 feet and at most 24 feet wide. The gates are placed so that the competitors can distinguish them clearly even at high speed. The gates are marked with red and blue flags in alternating order. Each gate has two flags.

PRESEASON TRAINING

You can't be a racer unless you're in shape. Without physical toughness, there just cannot be any mental toughness, and

Summer ski racing camps mean exercises, too. *(Bob Beattie Enterprises)*

Future ski racers are trained at summer camps. *(Curtis Casewit)*

the racer needs both. That's why the true young ski racer cycles, climbs, hikes, sprints, and rope skips all summer. In fall, some junior teams work out beyond an individual's point of exhaustion. This can be pure torture, and both girls and boys are expected to do their part.

As far as calisthenics are concerned, you can start your workout with some jumping jacks. Then some stretching exercises from the waist and trunk rotation. Now kick one leg up and touch your hand. Do half knee bends, leaping as high as you can. Roll on your stomach, do sit-ups, push-ups. These exercises should be done very day. Seniors add two more hours—*during which they cannot pause for a minute.* They do chin-ups, rope pulling, half knee bends, full knee bends, tumbling, broad jumping, more high jumping. This diet is followed by workouts that imitate actual skiing: you hop in and out of a series of automobile tires that are flat on the ground. You jump down from benches, which makes for sturdier legs. To copy slalom motions, you dart through trees.

HOW TO WIN RACES

Ask fifteen coaches about tactics and you usually get the same fifteen answers. Here are some good tips:

- Plan to be ready mentally before you even arrive at the race. As you build through training you can build up even more. Know your line and have complete confidence in it. This will reduce your stress.
- Build up your speed as you practice on a downhill course. Depending on the general snow conditions, the first run each day will find the course in the best shape. This is the time for the fast training runs once you are completely familiar with the course.
- Be aggressive. The best way to learn a downhill is by running it. Watching others is a poor second. For slalom you must attack, too.

Never downhill race beyond your ability. Every year, some of the boldest teenage downhillers gather for training camps in Colorado and California. Here they can imitate the nation's best downhillers and listen to coaches. Many of these youngsters still don't have the technical know-how to manage steep bumps at high speeds. Yet they see an Olympic racer stream downhill at 60 mph. Because they have courage, they do it, too. A bad bump can toss daring teenagers so high into the air that they can no longer land safely. The G-forces make you wind up 100 feet below with a possible sprain or fracture.

SKI JUMPING

High up, the young ski jumper pushes off and sinks into a crouch, chest against his knees. He speeds up in the two steep snow grooves toward the platform. Suddenly, his body uncoils, straightens, dives upward. He is airborne. Seconds tick away. The spectators gasp. Still he soars through the sky, then a smooth landing. Judges note the distance. The audience claps.

Young ski racers assemble for an award ceremony. *(Winter Park, CO)*

This winning boy expresses real pride on his face. *(Loveland Basin Ski Area, CO)*

Ski jumping is sensational to watch.

You may at once wonder about safety. Could you get hurt here? Ski jumping is much safer than downhill skiing. For one thing, the special hills are well prepared. For another, you jump in a straight line, and training is worked out with great care. Few young jumpers suffer serious accidents.

Before being taken on, you must know how to ski at least a little. There would be no point in learning to jump if you cannot come to training for many weekends. You first learn the basic aerodynamic position for the "inrun," meaning the short chute spurt before takeoff. You're taught the precise instant for leaping. You're shown how to stop safely and gracefully. In between there are various exercises. When you are ready to make actual jumps, you always start with the smallest hill. You only fly for a few feet here, but you get an idea of what it's like.

A few jumps later, you graduate to bigger hills, where you can zoom 30, 40, or more feet. In all, the typical ski resort has seven jumping installations. The largest, which is only for teenagers, allows distances of 170 feet; here speeds of 55 mph are normal.

The jumping meets pack the greatest excitement, both for the young athletes and for the spectators. The judges sit sternly in a tower, ready to compute results.

The young jumpers are judged not only by what distances they can reach, but also by their style. They lose points, for instance, by standing straight after takeoff. (You must be forward while in flight.) They lose points if their skis flutter in all directions. (The skis should be together.) They cannot win if their arms go like windmills. And they're evaluated for their landing–which should be steady–and for the ease of coming to a halt (no hands).

USEFUL ADDRESSES FOR RACERS

The U.S. Ski Association chapters help young racers in many ways. Here are the addresses:

Central Division–USSA
P.O. Box 66014, AMF O'Hare
Chicago, IL 60666

Rocky Mountain Division–USSA
1463 Larimer Square
Denver, CO 80202

Southern Division–USSA
P.O. Box 801
Belmont, NC 28012

Eastern Division–USSA
22 High Street
Brattleboro, VT 04201

Far West Ski Association–USSA
1313 West 8th Street
Los Angeles, CA 90017

433 Natona Street
San Francisco, CA 94103

Pacific Northwest Division–USSA
P.O. Box 6228
Seattle, WA 98188

WHERE TO GET COACHING IN SUMMER

Corrock Summer Race Camp at Grand Targhee, WY (Emphasis on technique, training. All ages.)

Red Lodge International Summer Racing Camp, Red Lodge, MT 59068 (All ages.)

Sailer Summer Ski Camp at Whistler Mountain, British Columbia, Canada (All ages.)

Rossignol Racing Camps, Williston, VT 05495 (Ages eight to eighteen.)

Taos Summer Racing at Taos, NM 87581 (All ages.)

Timberline Summer Racing Camp at Timberline Lodge at Mount Hood, OR 97028 (Ages nine to nineteen.)

CHAPTER 9

Snowshoeing

RETURN OF AN OLD SPORT

The scene is a Saturday morning near Stowe, Vermont. The first rays of the sun redden the snow. Nothing seems to stir in this winter landscape. Then comes complete daylight—bright, golden, topped by a flawless sky.

A few human figures assemble quickly down the road from Stowe's last houses. The people carry snowshoes that will allow them to enter New England backcountry.

By 9 A.M. forty snowshoers stand ready, almost twice as many as the Mountain Club leader had expected. Some of them are adults; some are teenagers.

Snowshoeing has made a strong comeback all over the United States and Canada. Snowshoe manufacturers find that the supply cannot always keep up with the sudden demand for snowshoes. All over New England, groups of snowshoers, some of them former skiers, set out into the wilderness. The Green Mountains, the White Mountains, the Laurentians all experienced a rebirth of this old method of moving about mountains in winter. West Coast enthusiasts head for the Sierra Nevadas, where snowshoeing was made famous by numerous Old West mail carriers, some of whom later used skis for greater speed. Back in the 1850s and 1860s, one route led from Placerville, California, to Carson City, Nevada, which took about a week for the round trip.

Snowshoes came in good stead when explorer Calvin Rutstrum roamed the frozen North, too. "A heavy wind was driving the snow horizontally," Rutstrum wrote. "The storm raged all day with relentless fury. The snow was getting much too deep for the dogs. From that point on, the trip would have to be on snowshoes."

One of the oldest inventions, snowshoes may rank in importance with the wheel. Archaeologists have not been able to pinpoint when or where the snowshoe was invented. But the best evidence indicates that the first pair showed up in Central Asia as early as 4–5000 B.C. Early man was thus able to hunt in the winter.

North American Indians, known for their innovative designs, developed the shoes for hunting. Some of today's best and least expensive models are actually manufactured by Indian communities.

Mother Nature fashioned snowshoes for many of her woodland creatures. The Bearpaw design got its name because of the resemblance to the bear's large and long feet. If you hike a lot in the winter, sooner or later you're likely to come across the tracks of a snowshoe hare, whose long legs enable him to stay atop of the white surface. Some types of birds (like the ruffed grouse) grow feathers around their feet for the winter months, to give them support.

SOME GOOD REASONS

Why is this sport "in" again? The reasons are easy to understand. For one thing, snowshoeing is just winter hiking. You don't need any lessons; you learn to walk in minutes with your webbed contraptions. And any age can play.

The feeling of exploration seizes even the average snowshoer. Ask a friend who has tried it. You'll hear about the contact with the land, a contact that can be lost by the downhill skier, who goes too fast to see the scenery. The snowshoer moves at a slow pace, and every detail emerges sharply.

A midwesterner wrote in her diary about her first excursion: "The scenic rewards are great. All evidence of man is swept under a deep, sound-absorbing blanket of white. Each pine cone, every spruce branch stands out clearly. Nature is always there. Behind me, the snow was blowing from the peaks; ahead, the sun shone through the trees." At another point, however, she admitted: "Thigh muscles shriek in agony."

It's true that unless you're in top shape, the first trip will mean some muscle pains. Snowshoes weigh several pounds, and every step means a workout for your legs. But that passes quickly. Indeed, here is a leisure-time activity for very young children, too. David Duffey, a well-known New England enthusiast, started his son and daughter when they were four years old. Vermont families go with babies on their backs. Many outdoor organizations–the Colorado Mountain Club serves as one example–offer Sunday snowshoe trips, which are popular with many different-aged groups.

The sport benefits your body.

Heart specialists will tell you that leg veins have valves to maintain circulation. Good muscle tone helps squeeze these veins. The valves insure that the blood goes one way, back toward the heart. The better the condition of the leg muscles, the better the circulation, the less work your heart has to do.

Fans also point to the safety record of snowshoeing. In a typical Pacific Northwest group, for instance, some of the most physically fit members admitted that they liked snowshoeing because fractures, and even sprains, were next to impossible. If you fall, the "harness" (or binding) lets your foot go at once.

Snowshoeing lets you relax from the hurried city life. The snowshoe trip succeeds because not every family can afford the often jammed ski areas.

SOME SPECIFICS

One of the nicest things about snowshoeing is that it requires practically no investment. You can usually rent a pair of shoes for less than the price of a meal. (Army and Navy or bigger sporting goods stores sell the gear cheaply.) Try a rental first; it gives you an idea about the sport, and helps you decide which type of shoe will be right for you.

Unlike other winter sports, snowshoeing takes only a minimum of time. No long drives are necessary; no full days are required. These winter hikes on webbed supports can be done, at first, in a few hours. A short afternoon will do fine. Organize a little party. Gather your parents, brothers, sisters, and hike to a summer campsite. You can build a small fire to cook your lunch and warm up before the return trek. (Just make certain that the fire is out when you leave.)

There are also certain essential precautions. First of all, never set out alone.

Secondly, turn back if the weather changes for the worse; otherwise, there may be trouble.

Thirdly, for those snowshoers who move at higher altitudes: learn something about (and beware of) killer avalanches. In a report written for a U.S. Forest Ranger, a snowslide victim described the encounter: "I was tossed around and engulfed immediately. It seemed as though I was in a big flume of water, and just occasionally able to get a breath of air. Most of the time I was overwhelmed by snow! Several thoughts ran through my head, one being that I was a damned fool for coming here, and secondly that I was sure to die."

This could have happened to anyone who ventures into the high mountains to snowshoe. Entire books have been written about western slides and where they occur. The precautions are simple: Watch for steep slopes. Beware of masses of fresh loose snow. Don't walk under cornices. (For more details, read the last chapter of this book.)

Experienced snowshoers carry extra strips of rawhide and one extra binding just in case a shoe should break. (You'd be helpless in the wilderness.) Ski poles can be useful on longer trips. Dressing warmly and adequately is another basic rule, about which you will read more later. Bring a pair of sunglasses even if the sun hides behind the clouds.

Old-timers will remind you that the equipment should be first tested at home. Most bindings need adjustments. Do it ahead of time, at home. Nothing irritates a trip leader more than having to stop every 50 feet while somebody works on the harness.

Snowshoers agree that on the whole, you don't do much better than 2 to 3 miles per hour. The record was achieved in Quebec where marathon snowshoers raced 10 miles in sixty minutes.

Even cross-country skiing on narrow Scandinavian boards usually achieves greater speeds than snowshoeing. On at least one occasion, however, two groups of average mortals started out from the top of Berthoud Pass, Colorado. Half the people—none of them racers—wore cross-country skis. The other group was on snowshoes. They were all headed toward a farm 6 miles downhill. Who arrived first?

Not the skiers. They'd fallen too much.

SELECTING YOUR SNOWSHOES AND EXTRAS

It's a simple matter to choose a pair of snowshoes. The shape and material may vary, but all of the models consist of a frame, usually made of wood, connected to some lacing. The binding is uncomplicated. Take several factors into consideration when choosing shoes. For example, what is your height and weight? Are you going to use the shoes for backpacking or just recreation? Is the terrain flat, open, with trails or forests? What are the snow conditions? Deep, light powder, soft or crusty?

Some thought must be given to the shape of snowshoes. For short hikes, the oval or round Bearpaw would be your best bet. The design makes it easy for beginners and works well in the woods and brush. The Bearpaw shoe is the most popular among hunters and fish and game departments.

The Bearpaw is not suitable for long distances across country, though. The Michigan or Northland type is an excellent all-purpose snowshoe. Developed by the Indians, this style is popular for both backpacking and hunting and supports weight better than any other model. The addition of a tail offers less drag than the Bearpaw models and acts as a stabilizer. Well-suited for just about all snow conditions and terrain (except thick brush), the Northland may be a little more difficult to master.

You needn't know much more about the various types. But a few rules of thumb can come in handy. If you're a newcomer to this activity, you'll find a more narrow snowshoe easier to maneuver. A longish, even more narrow "cross-country" snowshoe allows more speed and therefore encourages greater distances. The lighter a shoe, the further you can go without fatigue.

A slight uptilt in the front makes for easier walking in deep snow. If you do a lot of "bushwacking" (walking through brush), you'll find the going better on a short pair. One other rule: the harder the snow, the smaller the necessary shoe.

Snowshoeing can be more than just exploring the outdoors. These young people are actually racing in shoes. *(Canadian Government)*

If you plan on moving over flat ground, try a model in a teardrop shape. The broad and slightly upturned nose and a long and narrow tail enable you to walk along trails or through open wooded areas.

A pair of snowshoes will last the average person forever and it's unusual to wear out two pairs in a lifetime.

As far as lacing materials go, according to a Vermont manufacturer, rawhide is still a favorite among sportspeople and recreational snowshoers. The rawhide shoe is more abrasion-resistant and therefore lasts longer. Neoprene, a synthetic material, represents the first material change in several hundred years. While not as pretty as rawhide, neoprene resists snow buildup and is lighter than rawhide under wet snow conditions.

You'll find all kinds of plastic shoes on the market. These are fine for young people. A well-known western guide named Jim Petrie tested them. "One of our tests was on a fourteen-thousand-foot peak," he says. "The snow cover was thin. Rocks and stumps made for rough terrain. It would have wrecked conventional rawhide shoes. Yet the new plastic ones came through with flying colors." Petrie actually recommends snowshoes for winter mountaineering. In fact, many hardened climbers like to take a pair along, just in case.

The same shoes also serve winter fishermen, telephone linemen, utility men, foresters, zoologists. All can reach snow-blocked areas. Young people use them because they're extra cheap and lighter than their ash-wood counterparts.

There are two different types of bindings. The "H" style has an across-the-toe leather pad, a strap around the heel plus a strap around the instep. This type has only one drawback: the leather can stretch when wet, so you must occasionally retighten the harness. The other binding is made of plastic, which stretches less frequently under moist conditions. The cost for such a harness is slightly higher; some of the more popular models come with three buckles and a toe cap, which holds your foot well.

That's about all the equipment you need. Ski poles can be very useful for backing up and hurdling obstacles like fallen trees. Poles give you downhill support when traversing a hillside, and come in handy if you fall. But poles are not *required* for these situations and, if you need anything, a simple walking stick will often do.

The best type of boot is the one that keeps your feet the warmest. The inside should be loose enough to let you wear two or three pairs of socks. Your hiking or climbing boots with Vibram soles and steel shank arches should be ideal for a day hike. Snowmobile boots are perhaps the most functional and the cheapest. They usually have a felt inner-boot lining, rubber bottoms and sides, and either nylon or leather gaiters, which keeps the snow from entering from the top. Forget about tennis or street shoes. Last item: Bring some spare socks.

HOW ABOUT CLOTHES?

Fortunately, you do not need to spend a lot of money on clothing to enjoy this sport. Fashion is absent from snowshoeing. You need only be warm. A comfortable old sweater, a favorite parka, a wool shirt, a plain cap, your old pair of pants, and a pair of long underwear will do nicely.

Layered clothing, preferably loose fitting and of wool, is your best bet. Wool is warm, yet breathes well; it's tough and serves as a good windbreaker. It's water-resistant, but if it becomes wet (unlike any other material) wool will retain your body heat.

The advantage of layered clothing is that you can peel it off as you get warmer.

What else do you need for an outing? Besides your lunch, carry some high-energy food such as chocolate and nuts, a compass, waterproof matches, a flashlight, sun lotion, a first-aid kit, and mittens or gloves. All these things should fit neatly in a day pack and will hardly be noticeable on your back.

THE BASIC ABC'S OF SNOWSHOEING

Unlike skiing, where you must become familiar with the technique, snowshoeing requires mostly good legs. If the snow is right, you can use your leg strength and body weight for excellent snowshoe descents. (Experts call the method "glissading.")

As you start out, the shoes feel awkward. It will take about fifteen minutes until you get used to the wide stance required for walking. (If you walk normally, your pants will be in the way.) You'll eventually learn to raise your feet as little as possible. After half a mile you won't step on top of your own shoes.

This winter sport can generally be mastered on the first outing. Compare the gait to shuffling along your bedroom floor in a pair of houseshoes. Walk with a wide stance. Don't step on top of your own shoes. When you start out, it is a good idea to practice lacing your shoes. Take the first steps on level ground. This will help you get more enjoyment from your trip.

Keep the initial trips short. The first time a young New Mexico secretary went snowshoeing she found that she took as many rest periods as walking periods. She came home exhausted with one well-learned lesson: don't overdo it the first time.

A beginner should not be the first person to travel through deep snows. Let a more experienced person go ahead. This strategy makes sense. The expert breaks trail for the others who follow.

Most beginner groups restrict trips to 2 miles. Avoid the long journeys that are popular with some ambitious outdoorsmen.

Finding a gentle slope that leads to an open area has two advantages. You get an added appreciation of the scenery and a less tiresome experience on your first try. An even pace is better than a too-hurried one with a lot of rest stops.

You should *never* go snowshoeing alone. Go with at least

three other persons, including one seasoned snowshoer. In case of emergency, that person will know what needs to be done, or, if necessary, send someone for help.

Map out an unknown route beforehand on cross-country trips. You can buy topographical maps at some sports equipment outlets or the U.S. Forest Service offices. No one wants to get lost in the woods.

But just in case you do, plan to carry a survival kit, food rations, canteen, flashlight, waterproof matches, and snowshoe repair kit for day-long treks. Snowshoe repair kits are easy to assemble: Include a strong, pliable wire, rawhide lacings and thongs, a pocket knife, about 100 feet of ⅛-inch nylon cord, a pair of lightweight pliers, and adhesive tape (electrical tape will do).

HOW TO MAKE YOUR OWN SNOWSHOES–(THERE ISN'T MUCH TO IT)

Making your own snowshoes has two basic advantages. In addition to being fun and not difficult, it's a lot cheaper than buying a pair. Besides, you can get back to Mother Nature by using natural materials like saplings, branches, and vines. Some people use bark for their bindings, but remember that stripping a tree of all its bark will kill the tree. Vines or rawhide are much more efficient.

Begin with a sapling. Willow is your best bet, or any bendable, tough wood. Ash, though not easy to find, is traditionally used by commercial manufacturers. When steaming and shaping it into a snowshoe frame, ash maintains the proper curves. When you select the young tree, be sure and pick one that not only meets your needs, but also helps thin out a forest.

Cut your sapling–not more than 6 feet long–to make an oval of about 14 inches. You form the frame by cutting a 10-inch taper on both ends of the sapling, then lacing the ends together. The toe of the shoe is the lower end of the sapling.

A strong stick will strengthen the back of your snowshoe and help keep its shape.

A foot rest can be constructed from strong, unbendable branches to go under the balls of your feet. To fasten it across the frame use ropes, vines, or wire. You'll need a binding to hold your foot onto the snowshoe. It can be made in horse bridle fashion and fastened to your foot rest. First, loop a rope for your toes. Slip your toe into the loop. The ankle should be held by an additional piece of cord.

The webbing is one of the final jobs. Vines, rope, wire, or any twistable material is suitable. The mesh need not be elaborate. A random pattern will do. Make sure the webbing is tightened securely–without straining the frame–to avoid shifting.

WHERE TO GO

There are innumerable places one can snowshoe in the United States and Canada. Unlike skiing, snowshoeing requires only a light cover of snow. Whether you decide to go to the Green Mountains, the White Mountains, the Laurentians, or the Rockies, you'll usually find enough of a base.

Some of the best country is found in the immense national and state park systems. You can go almost anywhere on snowshoes. Up the steep winter meadows of the Canadian Cordilleras. Across the gentle mounds of Michigan, over Wisconsin hillocks, in the deep-snow regions of Utah. On a flat Appalachian trail. Just about any paths used for summer hiking can be used for snowshoeing.

If you live in the Northeast, you can reach one or more sections of the 2,000-mile-long Appalachian Trail. Start on Mt. Katahdin, Maine, for instance. Follow the snow-covered, highland terrain south over Sugarloaf Mountain (4,237 ft.). Take the trail to Spaulding Mountain shelter near the northwest end of the Mt. Abraham ridge of the Appalachians.

Snowshoeing can lead to winter tenting and backpacking. *(Quebec Tourist Branch)*

On the East Coast try Acadia National Park with Mt. Cadillac (1,530 ft.), the highest point on the Atlantic shoreline. Head through the beautiful, dense woodlands of Massachusetts and Connecticut. All these areas have hundreds of paths and unexplored wonderlands.

New York offers the Catskills as well as several state parks with fine trails for any type of outdoors person. Try Bear Mountain or Harrison State Parks; or Greenwood Lake near the New York/New Jersey border. In Pennsylvania, you can go just about anywhere in the Pocono Mountains. Remember, you only need a little snow cover.

Try the Allegheny National Forest in the northwestern part of Pennsylvania, or Kittatinny near the Delaware Water Gap National Recreation Area. On the New Jersey side of the Delaware Water Gap, there are three separate trails you could take to the top of Mt. Tammany (1,552 ft.), overlooking the Delaware River. In southern New Jersey, the Batona Trail encourages a winter walk through the Wharton State Forest. Several roads cross the trail at various points, which makes for interesting side trips. But don't attempt it all in one day; the trail itself is nearly thirty miles long.

Moving into the Midwest, the true adventurer will find many places to explore. For example, there is the Ohio River Valley of Ohio and Indiana. And, of course, the Ozarks, a heavily forested range that follows the Mississippi River Valley from southern Illinois down through Missouri.

Michigan's two peninsulas provide a wide range of territories from the Porcupine Mountains in the Northern Peninsula to the gentle slopes and cross-country tableland of the Southern Peninsula. Further north in Quebec, Canada, there are a number of nature-appreciation trails for the snowshoer. Try Mont Tremblant Park or Joliette Park. In the St. Maurice Valley, there is Mastigouche Park.

The ridges and hills of Wisconsin's rolling plains give the young snowshoer several opportunities to investigate the winter countryside. For example, hike up Sugar Bush Hill (1,951 ft.) in the Northern Highland district. Or trek through the 1,800-foot Penokee Range.

Down in the Southwest, Arizona and New Mexico, perhaps surprisingly, feature some excellent areas also. Head up to Tucson's winter oasis, Mt. Lemmon. In mideastern Arizona, the Sunrise ski complex contains some off-trail, forested areas just right for your handmade Bearpaw shoes.

Santa Fe and Taos in New Mexico are well-known mountain areas. In the same general region, but not as crowded, you find Sandia Peak and Los Alamos.

The mountain states, packed with national parks and forests, yield their vast beauty to snowshoers. Wyoming, for instance, is made up of some spectacular scenery known as the Yellowstone and Grand Teton National Parks. Or head for the Medicine Bow and Sierra Madre ranges in the central part of Wyoming.

The state of Colorado rivals Maine for the best and most scenic snowshoe terrain. The Front Range contains the vast

Rocky Mountain National Park where you could traverse one of the highest roads in the country, Trail Ridge Road. From here you'll see Long's Peak (14,255 ft.).

Colorado's main range is found in the western chain of the Rockies. Here, the snowshoer can hike over dozens of snow-bound roads that are only open the summer months of the year. In the Saguache Range, Mt. Elbert (14,431 ft.) dominates the view. There are also the Elk and Gore ranges and the San Juan Mountains. These and other ranges in the Colorado Rockies boast fifty-four peaks exceeding 14,000 feet in elevation.

Further west, you'll come to the high plateaus like the White River or Uncompahgre, and the descending gorges and canyons carved by the Arkansas River and her tributaries. These areas will all make for good hikes in the winter months.

Utah, also part of the Rocky Mountain group of western states, is divided by the picturesque Wasatch Mountains. Explore the Unita Range, the only major chain of mountains in the United States that extends from east to west. Utah has three national parks, two of which would be good for snowshoeing. Zion, located in the southwest corner of the state, has many easy trails. Brycc Canyon (in south central Utah) is another good destination.

Idaho presents a lot more than potatoes to the winter sportsperson. Among the major ranges of the Rockies passing through Idaho are the Bitterroot, Cabinet, and Sawtooth Mountains. You'll have a good chance spotting some of the many varieties of big game animals abounding in the national forests.

Up in the Big Sky country of Montana, Glacier National Park adjoins Waterton Lakes National Park in Alberta, Canada. Together they form the Waterton-Glacier International Peace Park. This mountainous land throughout the northern part of Montana contains nearly fifty glaciers, hundreds of lakes, and incredible views.

Down south again, try the contrasting variety of altitude

and terrains in the Mt. Charleston Range near Lee Canyon, Nevada. Or cross the state and move into the well-known Sierra Nevadas.

Continuing west into the Pacific Coast states, you'll find some of the best snowshoe country in the Mammoth Mountain area of California, about eight hours north of Los Angeles. In the High Sierras, try Heavenly Valley or Squaw Valley.

The northern extension of the Sierra Nevada is connected with the northern Rockies in Canada by the Cascade Mountains. This heavily wooded chain parallels the coast and has several snow-blanketed peaks over 10,000 feet. This includes the Mt. Hood (11,245 ft.) and Mt. Jefferson (10,200 ft.) areas in Oregon and Mt. Rainier National Park in Washington. You'll find mountain peaks, more than 150 active glaciers, and numerous canyons to investigate on your snowshoes in North Cascades National Park, Washington. And don't forget the wilderness areas of the Olympic Mountains.

Among snowshoers, you'll often hear how much they care for the environment. "We don't disturb nature on snowshoes," they say. "We don't upset ecology." That's what makes the sport different from skiing, especially the kind done at resorts. Snowshoers demand no cutting of trees, no bulldozing of ski boulevards, no base lodges with noisy parties.

The greatest use of the snowshoe remains purely that of recreation. There are few sports that offer as many benefits at so little cost. When you get into the wilderness, you can slowly feel your mind and body relax. Serenity fills your whole being. You are at peace with the world and yourself. You will be glad you're out there.

CHAPTER 10

Snowmobiling

WHAT'S GOOD ABOUT THIS SPORT

A snowmobile? The perfect name for the motorized vehicle that can travel on snow. Not quite as fast as a car perhaps, but fast enough. This sled on skis can reach 40 to 60 mph. The wind whips into your face. The snow flies behind you. You turn your throttle in the handlebar and roar uphill.

The snowmobile is an exciting invention that came to us from Canada in the late 1950s. Since then, many midwesterners have used these machines.

All across the United States "snow belt," there are families —once stuck at home in winter for lack of outdoor activity— using snowmobiles these days. The machine now allows people to reach their cottage far from plowed main roads.

A new dimension in picnicking has also been added. Unheard of a few years ago, the winter picnic has become commonplace. The snowmobile will get you to any favorite picnic retreat regardless of snow depths.

But perhaps the best thing about snowmobiling is this: Any youngster can do it. Age makes no difference. You need no license to drive a machine on private property.

There are two important points, however. If you're under eighteen, you're not permitted to snowmobile across roads, on roads, or on railbeds. (In some states you must complete a Snowmobile Education and Training program, or be accompanied by an adult.) In Canada, you need a driver's license to take machines onto authorized highways. Ski slopes or streets are out of bounds, too. You can ride only in designated areas, which include many mountain lands. To be safe, check with each state's snowmobile regulations. No sane adult ever allowed a youngster to steer a machine into the wilderness without at least one other snowmobile "safariing" along. (Other precautions will be discussed at the end of this chapter.)

WHY YOUNG PEOPLE ENJOY SNOWMOBILING

Why try snowmobiling? On the simplest level, it provides family adventure. You and your parents can ride a snowmobile across a sloping field, over a felt-soft meadow to inspect a frozen pond, or straight up a snow-covered mountain path to a lookout tower.

You can go fishing in winter, thanks to these jeeps on skis. You'll also welcome this Canadian invention if your family goes in for trapping or game viewing.

You may find it interesting that the Ski Patrol regularly uses snowmobiles at ski resorts to pick up injured skiers in the backcountry. The Eskimos in the Alaskan high regions often prefer the machines instead of sled huskies. (Indians use the name "iron dogs" for snowmobiles.)

Apart from serving kids of all ages as recreation, the mechanized sleds allow U.S. Forest Rangers to get into the snow-heaviest mountains. Says one western ranger: "We'd snowshoe in to mark timber. That used to be a two-day job. Now it can be done in half a day, thanks to the vehicles."

Or take the problem faced by rescuers of some 60,000 marooned Navajo Indians in Arizona. When the reservations were hit by one of the decade's worst snowstorms one winter, food, medical supplies, and hope ran out. A fleet of forty-five snowmobiles was flown from Denver to Gallup, New Mexico, complete with life-saving supplies. Snowmobiles have become so dependable that a team of motorized explorers pushed all the way to the North Pole and came back to tell the story.

One of the big attractions is snowmobiling as a sport, however. Like sports car buffs and boating fans, snowmobile enthusiasts are getting together to form clubs in many major snow areas. Typical of a club's activities are cross-country rallies, snowmobile races, a clinic to teach youngsters, and skijoring.

Skijoring originated in Scandinavia. Snow skiers are towed along behind a horse. In North America, the horse has often been replaced—by the snowmobile. A pair of snow skis, a 35-foot tow rope, and the machine will get you really ready for skijoring.

NOW THE BAD PARTS

"Those smelly, noisy things ought to be outlawed!" a television personality told millions of viewers some years ago. Snowmobiling, especially in mountainous country, has often earned a bad reputation and for good reasons. First of all, the machines consume fuel which will be scarce in the future. Secondly, snowmobilers *sit* on their trips through the hillsides. They don't use their feet like snowshoers or cross-country skiers. Like trail motor bikes, the mechanical sleds encourage laziness.

Some experts look at the future of snowmobiling with some fear. Will the wilderness resemble our interstate highways? Will the forests be full of turnpikes for snowmobilers? One man predicts that some day, snowmobiling may be complete with "passing lanes, traffic lights, and gas stations."

Many young people prefer their winter pleasures in quiet, mellow portions. Snowmobiles are noisy. They clang and rattle and fill your ears with cylinder explosions. The machines are unsuitable for persons who dislike mechanical things; the ski-cars have starting mechanisms, gears, transmissions, tank-like tracks and brakes. Much can go wrong with the engine. And a stalled 300 to 500-pound machine is not exactly everyone's idea of winter fun.

Snowmobiling! *(Bombardier & Co)*

In fact, snowmobiling is much more dangerous than cross-country skiing or snowshoeing or backpacking.

The mechanical breakdown is a real threat. Especially in cold weather. (That's why you should always be in company of someone else who can get help if needed.) Brakes have failed and throttles have frozen. Machines have tipped over, fracturing the rider's leg. Teenagers have suffered frostbite after their vehicle conked out. Drivers have been skewered by tree branches and cut by barbed wires. Snowmobilers even suffered broken backs by risking big jumps with their heavy machines. Riding across barely frozen mountain lakes, youngsters have broken through the ice and drowned. Each year, some snowmobilers get killed by trains and automobiles.

The sport takes plenty of brains if you don't want to get injured.

THE INJURED ENVIRONMENT

The biggest criticism is that snowmobiles damage the environment. Some snowmobilers chase animals, hunt from their machines, run over vegetation, or scare bystanders. Aerial studies of feeding patterns show that elk and deer are frightened of snowmobile noise and wander far from their normal grounds to avoid it.

In some states like Minnesota and Wyoming, drivers have harassed moose, elk, and deer. A frightened animal, weakened and hampered by winter snow, runs itself to exhaustion, stops, becomes seriously chilled, and dies of exposure.

It is also true that heavy use of a meadow in winter has an effect on the creatures who live under the snow. For instance, ground squirrels depend on snow cover to insulate them from cold and predators. A study showed that many of these animals die after the machines packed the deep snow under which they lived.

Studies also proved that heavy use of the terrain in winter damages the flora. How can machines hurt plants that are protected by a layer of snow? Scientists report that the snowmobiles change the nature of the snow itself.

Snow is a mixture of about ten parts air to one part ice. The air spaces between ice crystals in the snow insulate much like air spaces in goose down. As a result, snow traps the heat that radiates from the earth and keeps subsnow temperatures near or above freezing.

According to a study made by environment expert Russell Heath, snowmobilers destroy the insulating air spaces. As a result, two passages of a snowmobile increase the rate of heat loss through the snow four to five times. "The resulting colder temperatures kill or weaken plants living under the snow," writes Heath. "One machine has a greater effect than fifty snowshoers!"

HOW TO DRIVE THE MACHINE

Normal driving isn't difficult. Racing, on the other hand, makes for trickier handling and demands extra driving skills. The most important maneuver is the turn. It's a lot like a motorcycle; the more you lean into a turn with your body, the more you'll be able to bring the machine around.

Try a few "lazy 8s," as airplane pilots call them. These are two linked 360-degree turns of about 40-foot diameter. Go slowly at first, then build up speed in repeated runs until you start to feel the machine "slip" sideways. You'll find that even when it slips, or "breaks loose," you can control it either by easing off or increasing the throttle opening. A little experimentation will reveal just how much power you need for the snow conditions.

Now, try some "wiggle-waggles," a series of left and right turns along a straight course, just like a slalom skier. Make it a rule to plan ahead–even if it's only 500 feet ahead. When you drive up a hill, remember you've got to come down it, too. If the hill is very steep, you should have a good plan for how to come down. Your best method is to "traverse" down (or up) by making shallow "sweeps" across the face of the slope, progressing up or down about 30 feet with each sweep.

Test snow conditions before taking off on any ride. What was true of the snow yesterday isn't always true today, and an overnight freeze or snowfall can bring some surprises in the way you'll drive your machine. Try a few turns and stops. You'll get a better feeling of the trail, and you'll get more pleasure from the trip.

Lower your speed in unfamiliar territory, keeping an eye peeled for obstacles.

SNOWMOBILE ETIQUETTE AND RULES TO KNOW

Snowmobiling has been around for a long time now, so the industry has had the time to create a "Code of Ethics" for drivers, which includes you. Some of the important items in the Code:

- I will be a good sportsman. I recognize that people judge all snowmobilers by my actions.

- I will not litter trails or camping areas. I will not pollute streams or lakes.
- I will respect other people's property and rights.
- I will lend a helping hand when I see someone in distress.
- I will not interfere with or harass hikers, skiers, snowshoers, ice fishermen or other winter sportsmen. I will respect their rights to enjoy our recreation facilities.
- I will know and obey all federal, state, and local rules regulating the operation of snowmobiles in areas where I use my vehicle. I will inform public officials when using public lands.

Good snowmobile manners resemble those you observe as a hiker, backpacker, or camper: Courtesy does the trick. All this is simple enough. Drive your snowmobile in populated areas only during the hours when you know people are awake and not trying to sleep. Make sure you have permission to drive over privately owned land. Take care that gates are closed after you pass through them. Treat the privilege of using someone else's land respectfully. Do not drive on lawns . . . or on seeded fields. Look out for livestock. Do not disturb game herds. Respect fences.

DRESSING FOR WINTER

Snowmobiling calls for adequate protection against wind and low temperatures. Warmth, comfort, and freedom of movement should be your major considerations.

Begin with good-quality thermal underwear. Follow this with a pair of wind-resistant pants, a shirt, a bulky sweater (turtleneck is best), and a wind-breaking parka.

With the major portion of the body protected, three vulnerable areas—feet, hands, and eyes—need special attention.

Since the feet rest on your machine's running board, they don't get much exercise and can become cold. Choose waterproof thermal boots worn over two pairs of socks—one light pair over a heavier woolen set. Rubber-type boots are popular because of their foam insulation.

The well-dressed snowmobiler! *(Bombardier & Co.)*

Good control of the snowmobile requires warm, responsive hands. A pair of thick leather mittens are best, not only against the cold airstream, but also against snapping twigs and branches.

The cold winds demand proper eye protection. A pair of goggles with interchangeable lenses–gray or green lens for bright days, amber lens for cloudy days and late afternoon when flat light hides depressions in the snow–should be worn. In addition, goggles shield your eyes against lashing branches and twigs.

Finally, racing over snow at better than 30 mph dictates the use of some type of head gear, particularly over the ears. A stocking cap, snowmobile helmet, or hunter's hat with ear flaps are recommended.

SAFETY AND THE SNOWMOBILER

A few safety rules, given by the manufacturers, may be a good idea, too. For one thing, remember that few American states or Canadian provinces allow you to utilize regular highways. This makes sense because automobile drivers cannot see the too-low snowmobiles. For another thing, don't try hot-rodding.

Many parents have enough confidence to let their youngsters handle the steering.

Remember that snowmobiles are only in their element when running on *snow*. Really good snowmobiling requires about 6 to 12 inches of snow, or what might be called a medium snowfall. Extremely hard-packed or deep powder snow, or glare ice do not make an adequate base.

- Most snowmobiles are meant to carry two people: the operator and a passenger. Packing too many on a vehicle is like overcrowding a car. It just makes it harder for the driver.
- When you're cruising in the woods, watch for tree branches, snow-covered logs, or hidden depressions that could over-

turn your machine. Dips or holes can be almost invisible during the late afternoon, when the light goes "flat."

- On winter safaris, it's best to travel with another snowmobile. Long-range bush cruising is pleasant and challenging. You'll find it more comfortable with another machine along for company. Such a buddy system helps guard against getting lost or stranded if an emergency develops.
- Never touch freezing metal with your bare hands. You'll get blisters for your troubles. If your hand should become frozen to metal, pull it off gradually. The longer you're stuck, the deeper it freezes. Be especially careful with gasoline or oil cans.
- Nighttime is the most dangerous period of all for snowmobilers, because it is so difficult to see very far ahead. Slow down! A low-hanging branch or wire fence can easily melt into the background–until you hit it. Use your lights.
- Never tailgate! Avoid injury to yourself, to others, and to your machine by maintaining a safe distance between you and the vehicle in front. Handle your snowmobile at a sane, stoppable speed.
- Don't leave your key in the ignition. This is an invitation to theft and a danger to unsupervised younger children. The ease of electric starting is simple, even for a small child.
- Finally, always tell someone where you (and your friends) are going, and when you'll be back. A brief word or note to another person will help get you assistance, should you need it.

SNOWMOBILE RACING

Snowmobile drivers from all over North America assemble during January in the Canadian province of Quebec. At a signal, in teams, drivers straddle their machines. The motors explode into action. The men squeeze their handlebar throttles.

While thousands of spectators gasp, the competitors are blasting off on their motorcycles-on-skis. The racers cross forests, where other folks eye them. The competitors sweep over frozen rivers. At speeds of up to 60 mph they barrel across meadows.

Each season, snowmobile races are held from New York to Wisconsin and Michigan to California; some families have even traveled all the way from sunny Florida to Idaho, snowmobiles in tow. These contests are popular with spectators, too; the machines blast around barrels and engage in speed tests and marathon competitions.

Required equipment for a long race? Racers must have a crash helmet, pencil and paper (for emergency messages), a snow flap on the rear of the machine, cold-weather face mask, heavy winter snowsuit, matches, and a hunting knife. For long races drivers also carry first-aid kits, flares, and some spare parts for the machine.

The trails are marked by flags and snow dye. In some regions spotters stand along the way. Even airplanes sometimes circle the route.

Drivers must nurse their dogless snow sleds through any breakdowns or natural hazards.

If you want to watch a typical snowmobile race, here are a few: In December, there are races in West Yellowstone, Montana. For January, consider the "International Winnipeg to St. Paul '500' Marathon," and the Rhinelander (Wisconsin) Marathon. Laconia (New Hampshire) is the site for the Bourbon Cup championships, one of the highlights of the New England racing season, and New York State's championship is decided at Boonville. Some snowmobile clubs lay out cross-country or point-to-point races over distances as long as 40 miles. Some have run over 200 miles! Cross-country races should include as many types of terrain as possible.

HOW AND WHERE TO GET STARTED

The minimum age for racing varies. For now, you may just want to ride one of the machines for fun. Perhaps your parents own a snowmobile or have access to one through friends.

If you care to try one of these machines yourself, you can also rent them nowadays at many ski resorts or at gas stations.

To ride around your own private farmyard, no license is required in any of the states or Canadian provinces. In some states and provinces, you must be at least sixteen to rent and you may have to take a safety education course. It is best to inquire about local laws.

A special code applies to snowmobiling in our national parks.

Many superintendents require that you register as you enter and leave the area. Each superintendent can establish snowmobile rules as they apply to a park's particular environment. The lights must be on when the vehicle is used from a half hour after sunset to a half hour before sunrise (and at any other time when persons and vehicles are not clearly discernible for a distance of 500 feet). Racing and other competitive events are prohibited in national parks. If you're under sixteen, you can't operate a snowmobile unless under the direct supervision of an adult.

You'll need your parents' support and permission. It takes a big allowance to rent a machine for the weekend. Camping centers, ski lodges, sports shops, garages, snowmobile dealers, and even service stations often group together several families for outings.

Some snowmobilers also employ local guides into the backcountry. The guides teach you how to handle deep powder snow. They show you techniques for managing steeper terrain. And they know their area.

Fortunately, there are now thousands of marked trails in North America. In Minnesota, for instance, where snowmobiling is a way of life for young people, the state forests alone contain 1,800 miles of trails, mostly marked, so that you can't get lost. In addition, you can snowmobile on certain federal lands and often on private lands. Many of the snowmobile trails in Canada and the United States are actually kept up, just like ski trails, by special equipment. (The machines are known as "trail groomers.") Your parents may consider joining one of the many snowmobile clubs; these often organize outings, and the organizers know all the major trails in your vicinity.

Here are some useful addresses. Feel free to write these groups and ask for more information:

Canadian Snowmobile Association
38 rue St. Vincent
Ste. Agathe-des-Monts, Quebec, Canada

U.S. Snowmobile Association
101 Snowmobile Drive
Eagle River, WI 54521

American Snowmobile Association, P.O.
Columbia Heights, Minneapolis, MN 55421

International Snowmobile Association
734 15th Street, N.W.
Washington, DC 20005

National Safety Council
425 North Michigan Avenue
Chicago, IL 60611

CHAPTER 11

Other Mountain Sports

ENGINELESS SKIBOBBING: RIDING A BIKE ON SKIS

Is there a bicycle that can go on snow and ice? Puzzled motorists just couldn't believe it. Yet the action at the 12,000-foot-high Continental Divide stopped traffic. People watched as Coloradans were trying a new kind of motorless, noiseless skibob. Compare it to a bike on skis, complete with handlebars for steering, a saddle to sit on, and the ability to go as slow or fast as you please. After an hour of instruction, teens are shooting down the knolls on the snowbike.

You may never have heard about this mountain sport. The skibob has a ski in the back, plus a frame to hold it all together. Two wooden claws are strapped under your boot soles. These brakes allow you to slow down or stop any time you like.

Young people find a skibob easier to ride than a bike.

You just point it downhill and go at whatever speed you wish. Your travel seems as silent as the pillowed, white scene around you. Gravity is your motor, and even a preschooler can control the bob. (The saddle is only 1½ feet from the ground.)

Older teens like the handling ease. Even clumsy adults who wouldn't dare take up skiing find that an hour's practice is

Ski bobbing. *(Dick Smith, North Conway, NH)*

A group of ski bobbers in Austria's Alps. *(Austrian National Tourist Office)*

enough for a swing down the slope. You can run on packed snow as well as deep powder.

Falls are rare and harmless. The Austrians like to say: "Skibob fahren, Knochen sparen," which means: "Skibobbing? Bone-saving!"

Skibobbing always proved to be safer than skiing. Of 100,000 enthusiasts in the Alps, for example, only one broke his leg. This was during a race where the man rushed down a steep incline at 85 mph (the speed record is 102 mph). All the same, you must always stay in control of your snowbike.

For many years now, ski bikes have been seen in some American sports shops and ski-specialty houses. Adult models are expensive, but you can buy a junior skibob (ages six to thirteen) for less than a night's lodging at a resort.

Some practical fathers can actually convert an old bicycle for use on snow. You can also rent a skibob from some ski areas in New York, New Hampshire, Vermont, Massachusetts, Wisconsin, Utah, Colorado, and New Mexico. Some of the resort managers let you use their ski tows as the uphill transportation. Certain regions have also set aside special slopes for skibob riders. Canadians sometimes call skibobbing "bi-skiing."

Your parents can let you try out this sport in your hometown. Just rent a ski bike at a sporting goods store and go to a hilly city park. The wooden frame is not too heavy, so it can be carried up a small hill.

Skibobbing seems ideal for weaker youngsters because it doesn't require much physical effort. Nor do you need to be fit.

One Austrian expert recommends this skibobbing technique: "Keep your knees tight to the bicycle, elbows close to the body, and feet parallel to the bike. The skibob is constructed for maximum cushioning of shocks. Just lift yourself slightly out of the saddle as you navigate over bumps."

Keep in mind that this sport is different from skiing. Skibobbing offers fresh air and speed, but no great exercise. Unlike the skier, a skibobber hardly moves his legs, except for occasional braking. (Experts slow down by making turns.) Skiing is much warmer, too. On the way down a mountain face, a skier is in almost constant motion.

SKIJORING

Skijoring dates back several centuries. It came to us from the Scandinavian countries where the winters are long and the snow is deep. It simply requires one person on skis and another on a horse pulling you. (Or on a snowmobile.) Each member of the team is dependent upon the other. You might compare it to waterskiing.

At some winter carnivals, you can see drivers with such superb timing that the skier can pick up rings or other objects. The sport is included here because skijoring can be done in hilly country. In some areas, there are competitions between several skijorers.

TOBOGGANING, TUBING, AND OTHER DOWN-THE-HILL SPORTS

There are other winter diversions on hillsides. The newest idea, tobogganing, has been around a long time. But did you know that you could ride downhill on an inflated air mattress? It acts like a toboggan. You steer with hands and feet.

You can also zoom downslope on an old truck tire tube. Your father may have one stashed away in the garage or basement. Or go to a truck outlet, which sells a tube for a few dollars. Blow it up and head for the nearest park slope to join the sledders.

Tubing is safe enough if you first inspect the hill and pay attention to what you're doing. You should always be able to avoid collisions with your fellow-tubers and be capable of steering around rocks or other objects. At one western ski area, the sport was discontinued because too many careless youngsters got hurt.

You'll see many fiberglass toboggans on some slopes. These models can stand hard knocks.

Naturally, the genuine toboggan is more expensive than the truck tube or a kid's sled. Sledding can be a competitive sport; it is then know as "luging." Streamlined, well-built luges can be seen at the winter Olympics. (*Luge* is the French word for sled.)

Above the Olympic town of Lake Placid, New York, a bobsled run curves, pitches, and falls for a long, icy, downhill mile. Compared to luges, the bobsleds are true heavyweights at about 1,000 pounds or more. The bullet-shaped sleds have room for two riders (sometimes four). The bobsled rocks and screeches down the ice, and if you stand below, the timers can tell you the speeds. Eighty miles per hour is slow. One hundred is more like it. Occasionally, men are pitched off the sleds. This sport is not for amateurs.

BIRD WATCHING AMONG THE PEAKS

Some young people consider bird watching a mountain sport; it is enjoyable to get up the hillsides under your own steam and not on a snowmobile or in a jeep (which would scare away the birds). You can study birds in winter when certain species change the color of their feathers.

You can watch birds of all kinds in North America's higher regions. A single tree may be occupied by the nests of several species like a clan of mountain chickadees, a mountain bluebird, or a woodpecker, who builds a home for himself as well as for others. In your future mountain travels, you may see Alpine crows, black ravens, hummingbirds, larks, thrushes, and waterfowl, such as mallard ducks and Canadian geese, snow geese, all at various life zones. According to a Mt. McKinley naturalist, there are over 130 kinds of birds in the

National Park. The variety is staggering. In Yellowstone, Wyoming, you may spy white trumpeter swans, which are graceful, proud, rare, shy of humans.

The gray jay, or Canadian jay, is the opposite; not many feathered creatures are as bold. Various species of jays make their home in the New England mountains, in the Canadian Laurentians, and in the Pacific Northwest, Jays fly the peaks in British Columbia, Canada. The gray jay (also known as Rocky Mountain jay, or mountain jay, or "camp robber") is also a familiar sight on the pinnacles of the American West, particularly those that get some human traffic. One favorite site: the summit sundeck on Aspen mountain. Here a partially glassed-in oasis commands a fabulous view of Mt. Hayden and Castle Peak and several dramatic valleys. The sundeck is popular with summer picnickers, who enjoy the sun and the fresh air. Camp robbers often swoop from the nearest trees onto empty tables, winging away with some edible loot. The mountain bird's flight is as pretty as any sea gull's, and its appetite is just as varied. Jays pounce on leftover potato chips, apple peels, unfinished sandwiches, cookies. They like crackers of all kinds and eat meat. If there are no leftovers from picnics, jays get along well on various insects.

Birdwatchers are known as "birders." How do you become one? If your elders are not interested in taking you to the mountains, you may be able to join a class in your school; some of them take trips on weekends.

Also consider a local birding group or natural history society. They furnish contact and information through meetings, lectures, publications, and field trips. Some of such groups are members of the National Audubon Society.

Young people are welcome on most of the short trips, and certainly at the lectures and films.

Does a birder need special equipment? Not absolutely. But if you're serious about learning more, you'd be well-served by buying a pair of prism binoculars. Herb Saltford, a leading Audubon member, suggests that you ask for 6 to 8 power,

The outdoors in winter means sighting animals, too. *(Wyoming Travel Commission Photo)*

preferably with center focus. (Though 7 × 35 are most popular, 7 × 50 and 8 × 50 are often used.) Your parents can buy them at a camera store.

Clothing for the field depends on your circumstances and local conditions. Good walking or hiking shoes are a must. Take a sweater or a jacket to wear over a shirt. A hat provides warmth in case of cold.

"Don't wear bright clothing," advises Saltford, who lives in Poughkeepsie, New York. "Walk slowly and quietly–alone or in small groups." You can attract some birds by squeaking with lips against the hand, or imitating bird songs.

Make a note of two organizations that can send you more information:

The National Audubon Society
950 Third Avenue
New York, NY 10022

The American Birding Association
Box 4335
Austin, TX 78765

THE ROCK COLLECTOR/PROSPECTOR

To a geologist a mountain is gneiss, granite, schist, sandstone, limestone; a mass of sedimentary or metamorphic rock, worn away by streams and glaciers, perhaps weathered into piles of scree (small stones.) The junior geologist can examine the rock as well. All you need is a good book, a rock hammer, a magnifying glass. (Or you could bring a pan to sift through a mountain stream for its contents.)

Rocks make fascinating objects of study and are one good reason to hike in the high country. You will find many rock varieties and perhaps even valuable gems. (In the mountains of Montana, for instance, the rockhound may discover real rubies and moss agates.) If you look long enough, you may also see fossils; shells that date back to ancient seas which covered the mountains at one time.

Prospecting for gold is something that many young people dream about trying at least once. To the person who is mainly concerned with this activity as a vacation diversion, prospecting offers a special excitement. There is a constant hope that the next pan of sediment may be "pay dirt." No other thrill can compare when you see even a few tiny flecks of gold glittering in the black sand at the bottom of your pan. The search itself is its own reward. Panning is the easiest method of separating the gold from the silt, sand, and gravel of the stream deposits. Much of the prospecting is done in mountain streams. You won't make money by panning gold in the streams of the West, but you'll have an enjoyable time.

Prospecting is also done in shallow rivers of the Appalachians and other high country. If the waterway is somewhat deeper, you'll spot still other mountain sports enthusiasts. The kayakers, for instance, who paddle their slender boats through raging waters. You may see canoeists in mountain streams and lakes, as well as rafts of various kinds.

There seem to be almost as many mountain sports as there are mountain chains in North America.

CHAPTER 12

Mountain Dangers and Precautions

Wyoming's Grand Tetons always make a big impact. The magic world of mountains can be experienced strongly here.

You can take some ranges for granted, get used to them, hardly see them any longer. Not so the Tetons. You just can't overlook or become accustomed to them. Each time you face these big marbled peaks they dazzle the eyes. The Tetons shoot straight up from the Wyoming plains. Because you reach this impressive range only after much travel, you can be truly close to nature here. The climber shares the idyllic lakes and the sight of hidden waterfalls and the steep remote mountainsides with few other people.

Yet this beautiful country is full of hidden dangers. The Grand Tetons, like other high mountain chains, claim victims all year long. Most of the people were not aware of the perils that awaited them. Hikers get into bad weather without adequate clothing. Each year a climber dies of hypothermia; he freezes to death. A cross-country skier takes a wrong route in winter, to be swallowed, crushed by avalanches.

COPING WITH THE ALTITUDE

If you live in the flatlands of Kansas or Nebraska and fly to Colorado, you'll be affected by the altitude. During your first day, you will tire faster. You may feel lightheaded.

Most plains or sea coast people have some trouble with their breathing. A visitor from the East once described his own battle with the Continental Divide. "Your breath comes hard," he wrote. "The altitude really socked it to us. We were so tired we could hardly walk!"

If you start climbing to 14,000 feet, you will get only 75 percent of the oxygen available at sea level. Your pulse now races faster. Some newcomers to the heights lose their appetite and feel irritated or weak; others do not sleep well. Girls notice their skin becomes dry.

But your body will adapt to all these conditions at altitudes up to 14,000 feet. The higher you go, however, the slower you become and the greater the fatigue. An extended rest in bad weather could thus spell great danger. Indeed, any activity above 20,000 feet can result in lung problems or even total collapse. At this point, a quick descent from the mountain becomes as essential as bottled oxygen.

So what do you do about altitude? How do you cope with the changes? Mountain people say that you should take it easy at first. Don't put in a big climbing effort during your first day at 9,000 feet. Go to bed a little earlier. Avoid strenuous exercise on your second day, too. Get used to the elevations. To reach the top of their sea-level form, even Olympic athletes are reminded by their doctors that it takes about twenty-four hours to get accustomed to each 1,000 feet of elevation.

FATIGUE AND EXHAUSTION

Fatigue does not only affect the flatlander who tries to jog in the Rocky Mountain National Park on the day of his arrival. Fatigue can also trouble young people who live in the high country. In fact, fatigue can lead to total exhaustion. If you add severe weather conditions, death may result.

Strange as it may seem, you can perish in a very short period of time (as little as six hours) from hiking in wind and cold. A person away from civilization is wholly dependent upon a limited supply of usable energy and the insulation qualities of the body. Many outdoors people realize these real dangers.

Doctors know a great deal about the bodily changes that occur if you exercise in the high mountains. If you strain too hard you'll become exhausted. Unless you slow down at that juncture–or rest–you may not be able to keep in motion.

It all has to do with a number of important physical factors. First of all, your moving muscles burn up available energy reserves. Secondly, your body produces certain by-products that must be flushed out by resting. If a sudden change of weather forces drive you on, you won't have a chance to recover from the prolonged strain.

Rapid movement in the mountains will lead to sweating and loss of moisture (followed by dehydration). You'll lose valuable heat.

The maintenance of your body temperature actually depends on a delicate balance between heat loss and heat production. Chilling of your skin leads to an increase of heat loss; the fit person increases heat production by exercise or shivering and so maintains the balance. Once exhausted, however, you can no longer generate enough heat by exercise.

The first visible signs of exhaustion are poor reflex actions (stumbling, less control of arms and legs), the need for frequent and prolonged rest stops, and a dazed, careless attitude with shorter attention span.

HANDLING WEATHER EMERGENCIES

The mountain rescue groups agree on how to handle various mountain weather problems.

- Wind–cover all exposed parts of your body. Put on adequate clothing for body protection or find suitable natural shelter.
- Rain–keep as dry as possible, remain in shelter. Wet clothing causes excessive body heat loss. Keep firewood dry, especially tinder for signal fires.

- Blizzard–do not travel. Quickly find suitable wind and cold shelter. Remain until storm abates. Gather lots of firewood, and boughs for insulation.
- White-out–do not travel. Hole up in suitable shelter: in timber or snow trench if in exposed area. Keep insulation under you. Wait for clearing skies.
- Dense Fog–do not travel. Find suitable shelter.
- Darkness–do not travel. Improvise adequate shelter; wait for daylight.
- Lightning–leave high, exposed areas immediately; crouch down away from trees, caves, cliffs.

The combination of wind, snow, and cold can mean some extra hazards. One of these is known as the "windchill factor." As a mountain traveler in winter, you should know that the wind will lower temperatures. To illustrate: A wind speed of 30 miles per hour can drive a normal temperature of 5 degrees Fahrenheit down to minus-41 degrees!

Such cold weather increases your chances to suffer frostbite. You can prevent it by dressing adequately; make sure you wear warm mittens and keep your ears covered. (Did you know that you can lose 60 percent of your body heat through your head? Keep it covered for warm feet!) Ask a friend to watch your exposed skin for extreme whiteness and keep moving downhill and out of danger.

Frostbite can also occur at above freezing temperatures, especially if it's windy. Your hands may be thawed by placing them into your armpits; your ears by covering them with hands. Never rub the affected area; never put it near a fire or use snow. Instead, dip your frostbitten limbs into lukewarm water.

HYPOTHERMIA

If you get exhausted in the mountains, your inner body temperature begins to fall and exposure may result.

The next peril is known as "hypothermia," which can bring

progressive mental and physical collapse. Hypothermia begins with uncontrollable shivering, followed by the inability to maintain muscle movement. The exhausted person does not have the mental capacity to recognize these things. Be alert for them.

Oddly enough, hypothermia victims often feel fine. But they'll be drowsy, confused, sluggish. Their speech may not function. In severe cases, they'll lose their memory. Their skin turns blue.

To be sure, it is best to prevent the condition in the first place. Protect yourself against the rain. Wet undergarments are dangerous. Dress warmly. Turn back in bad weather. Or make camp while you still have a reserve of energy. Keep in mind that exposure greatly reduces your normal endurance.

On longer tours–in summer or winter–at least one member of your party should bring certain emergency items. The kit should contain candles, matches to make a fire, bouillon cubes for fresh energy, tea bags for a hot drink, and a space blanket for extra heat and for signaling to rescuers.

What if one of your party suffers hypothermia?

Get the victim out of the wind and rain.

Strip off all wet clothes.

If the victim is only mildly impaired, give him warm drinks. Get him into warm clothes and a warm sleeping bag. Well-wrapped, warm (not hot) rocks or canteens will speed recovery.

If the victim is semiconscious or worse, try to keep him awake. Give him warm drinks. Leave him stripped. Put the victim in a down sleeping bag. If you have a double bag, put the victim between two warm donors. Skin to skin contact is the most effective treatment.

WHAT TO DO WHEN GETTING LOST

Exhaustion and exposure can be the result of suddenly being lost in unfamiliar mountain terrain.

Here are some common-sense rules:

Stop! Sit down and try to figure out where you are. Use your head and not your legs. Your brain is the key to survival.

If caught by night, fog, or storm, stop at once and make camp in a sheltered place. Build a fire in a safe spot.

Do not wander about. Travel only downhill.

If you are injured, choose a clear spot, on a hill if possible, and build a signal smoke.

Do not yell, do not run, do not worry, and above all, do not quit.

Every mountaineer or person spending any time outdoors should know about the uniform distress signal. It is "three quickly repeated calls (audible or visual), repeated at regular intervals." The interval of time between calls depends upon the method of signaling. When using a flashlight or waving an object, the interval may be only one or two seconds. When using a whistle, the intervals should be longer. Wait long enough between calls for any echo or trace of the first signal to die out. Anyone hearing a distress signal must go to the assistance of the party in distress, or notify rangers, guides, or any person able to accomplish a rescue. It is desirable that people in the mountains refrain from yodeling, hallooing, or yelling. This is especially true where several separate parties make a difficult climb.

The Colorado Mountain Club has some excellent additional pointers on your priorities when lost:

To survive, you'll need:

1. Shelter from cold, wind, snow, and rain. If possible, retreat to timbered areas for shelter construction and fire. Utilize natural bridges on the windless side. Consider rock outcroppings, slope depressions, snow blocks, or a snow hole at the base of standing trees. Dense stands of trees. Under downed trees. Improvise wind break or shelter from natural materials: stack rocks or snow blocks. Use tree trunks, limbs, bark slabs, and evergreen boughs. Dig a snow cave or snow trench with cover.

2. You'll need warmth. To conserve body heat, put on extra clothing. Replace damp undershirt and socks. Place damp wool clothing over dry clothing. Loosen boot laces to increase circulation and place feet with boots in pack. Use equipment or ever-

green boughs to insulate yourself from ground. Place hands in armpits or crotch area. You can share body heat by sitting front to back or back to back. Warm hands and feet of an injured person. To create body heat, nibble high-energy foods like candy, nuts, bacon bar, or raisins. Isometric exercises can stir up circulation.

3. Fire-building skills in adverse weather. Skilled fire building comes through practice and experience. A properly prepared fire costs only one match. Wet wood burns as it dries in a strong fire. Gather dead, lower branches and bark from the dry underside of trees. Look under downed trees and inside dead logs. Cut dry portion away from wet wood for kindling. Select sheltered area protected from strong winds. Surround candle stub with branches to hold kindling over candle. Place hatchwork of kindling followed by slightly larger materials. Light a candle, the flame will dry and ignite damp kindling. Blowing lightly may help burning. Add additional light and medium materials to flame area. Feed end of logs and trees progressively into fire.

AVALANCHES

An avalanche is a snow mass that suddenly roars down a mountain slope, burying anyone in its path. Even small slides can be powerful.

It is easy to underestimate the speed of the white tonnage. In one classic case, a Walt Disney cameraman was dispatched to the Rockies to make a film about slides. The motion picture photographer persuaded the state highway authorities to shoot down an avalanche for him. Someone told the Disney man where he should stand. The photographer ignored the safety instructions. Suddenly 120,000 tons of snow thundered straight toward him, pulling up 80-foot-high trees, and killing the man.

The more time you spend in skiing, snowshoeing, snowmobiling, and other winter activities, the greater are your chances of being caught by snow avalanches.

Understanding the basic types of avalanches and the con-

This isn't a practice session to find an avalanche victim. Someone is actually under tons of snow. *(Curtis Casewit)*

tributing terrain and weather factors, as well as carefully selecting a safe route, can help you avoid being caught in a snow avalanche. It will also help you survive if you are buried in one.

Snow avalanches are complex natural phenomena. It is difficult to predict avalanche conditions with certainty. But some general guidelines will help you develop judgment about the presence and degree of avalanche danger.

There are two principal types of snow avalanches: loose snow and slab.

Loose snow avalanches start at a point or over a small area. They grow in size and the quantity of snow involved increases as they descend.

Slab avalanches start when a large area of snow begins to slide at once. There is a well-defined fracture line where the moving snow breaks away from the stable snow. Slab avalanches are characterized by the tendency of snow crystals to stick together. There may be angular blocks or chunks of snow in the slide. Knowledge can help you avoid being caught by a snow avalanche; it will help you survive if you are buried.

Avalanches demand special precautions in the Alps. Note the metal poles to hold the snow. *(Hans Truol)*

Many weather factors affect the possibility of a snow avalanche: temperature, wind, storms, rate of snowfall, and types of snow.

Snow persists in an unstable condition under cold temperatures. It will settle and stabilize rapidly when temperatures are near, or just above, freezing.

Storms starting with low temperatures and dry snow, followed by rising temperatures, are more likely to cause avalanches. The dry snow at the start forms a poor bond and has insufficient strength to support the heavier snow deposited late in the storm.

Rapid changes in weather conditions (wind, temperature,

snowfall) cause snowpack changes and cause an avalanche. Therefore, be alert to weather patterns.

Sustained winds of 15 mph increase the danger of an avalanche occurring. Snow plumes from ridges and peaks indicate that snow is being moved onto other slopes. This can create dangerous conditions.

A high percentage (about 80 percent) of all avalanches occur during and shortly after storms. Be extra cautious at these periods. Loose, dry snow slides with ease. Moist, dense snow tends to settle rapidly, but during windy periods can be dangerous.

Snow falling at the rate of 1 inch per hour or faster increases avalanche danger.

Always look for signs of recent avalanche activity and old slide paths. Listen for sounds and cracks; be alert to snow conditions.

The steepness of a slope is decisive. Experts distrust slopes of 30 to 45 degrees, but avalanches can also occur on inclines ranging from 25 to 60 degrees. Smooth, grassy slopes are considered more likely to slide than areas with big rocks, trees, or heavy brush that help anchor the snow. Sudden blizzards, windstorms, or a sudden rise in temperature may also add to the danger. In general, avalanches require at least 6 to 8 inches of new snow. If the temperature and the slope are right, danger may still exist several weeks *after* a heavy snowfall or blizzard.

Avalanches are often started by the needless rifle fire of hunters or by people testing their revolvers in mountain country. Even a loud yell can bring down a slide.

The outdoors person must be prepared for the menace. In fact, what do you do if you're caught in a slide? A Colorado U.S. Forest Ranger gives this advice: "Call out to the other members of your party. Let them know where you are in case you get buried. Dump your poles, skis, ice axe, and rucksack, if possible. Jump off your snowmobile. Make swimming motions. Try to stay on top; work your way to the side of the avalanche. Before coming to a stop, get your hands in front of your face and try to make an air space in the snow as you are coming to a stop.

If you are the survivor:

Mark the place where you last saw victims.

Search for victims directly downslope below the last seen point.

If they are not on the surface, scuff or probe the snow with a pole or stick.

You are the buried person's best hope for survival.

Do not desert victims and go for help, unless help is only a few minutes away. Remember, you must consider not only the time required for you to get help, but the time required for rescuers to arrive. After thirty minutes, the buried individual has only a 50 percent chance of surviving.

CREVASSES

A large glacier may not appear to be menacing. But a glacier comes with fractures known as crevasses. Some of these are concealed by snow. Under thin snow bridges, the hidden gaps may go down for 100 to 300 feet. That's why you're tied to your companions with a rope. A lone glacier climber can fall into a crevasse.

This happened to an American boy who left his parents on a glacier top to walk around alone. He wore slick rubber boots. He carried no ice axe, which, had he known how to use it, might have stopped his fall. After a ten-minute walk, the boy fell into the small crack. He got stuck 10 feet below the opening. The fissure narrowed like an hour glass. He tried to climb up again, but he slid all the way down to the bottom of the 20-foot crevasse. The American boy reached his chilly prison unhurt. He began to scream for help. He screamed for six hours until by chance a passing skier heard him and organized a rescue team. The ice dungeon would have surely killed the careless youngster that night.

Some victims are not found for months or even years, kilometers away from where they'd dropped out of sight. Professional guides and leaders of glacier expeditions, therefore, always remain on guard.

The dangers make it easy to understand why the experts say only thoughtless individuals tackle such terrain alone. In the French Alps, special guides pilot their clients safely past the gaping ice wounds of Europe's highest peak, the Mont Blanc. The crevasses are marked with red flags, and you must be able to turn skillfully on skis.

A FEW FIRST-AID HINTS

You may be hiking, climbing, snowshoeing, cross-country skiing for a lifetime without an emergency.

Yet an accident could happen. If there is no adult along, you'll want to know what action to take. Faced by an emergency in the wilderness, young people in their early teens have often done the right things and saved lives.

If you travel a lot in the mountains, you may want to take a First Aid course. It's free; you need only contact the American Red Cross. Any youngster over the age of thirteen may take the standard First Aid course.

The American Red Cross will instruct you on how to handle injury cases. Among other things, you'll learn about the following:

Injury	*Symptom*	*What to do*
Bruises	Red and blue marks on skin	Rest injured part. Apply cold compresses for half hour (no ice next to skin). If skin is broken, treat as a cut.
Scrapes	Skin is scraped or scratched	Use wet gauze or cotton to sponge off gently with clean water and soap.

Injury	*Symptom*	*What to do*
Cuts	Can be slight or deep	Wash with clean water and soap. Apply sterile gauze dressing. If need be, press firmly to stop bleeding. Bandage. Obtain medical care for deep, jagged, or extensive cuts.
Slivers	Redness	Wash with clean water and soap. Remove with tweezers. Wash again.
Severe bleeding	Blood gushes	Direct pressure to bleeding area. If bleeding persists, apply pressure to artery between wound and heart.
Fractures	Look for deformities. Compare victim's limbs. Compound fracture has wound as well.	Call a physician. If none is available, make splints with branches, cardboard, or other objects.
Fracture	All broken bones can cause severe pain.	See above.
Sprains	Redness, swelling	Elevate injured part. Apply cold compresses for half hour. Use ace bandage. If swelling is unusual, suspect fracture and treat as such.
Shock	Weak pulse; shallow breathing, cold skin. May be unconscious.	Stretch out patient horizontally. Assure warmth by means of extra blanket or sleeping bag in winter. Keep cool in summer. Get help.

The possibility of getting hurt underlines the importance that you never go into the mountains alone. A party should consist of at least three people. Take along a small first-aid kit, available at any drug store. After an accident, consult a doctor.

RESCUES

It is not likely that you'll get involved in a rescue operation. But if you do, you should know what is involved.

The right attitude is important. Keep calm and don't lose your head. The injury of one member need not endanger the others. The leader must make sure, though, that the others in your party are safe. Get out of the way of another rock fall, avalanche, or other unsafe situation.

In some minor injury cases, you may be close enough to a village or town to transport the patient there. If the person is unable to walk, you can improvise. Build a stretcher. Use

Modern ski patrol takes care of accident victims. *(Peter Runyon, Vail, CO)*

pack frames, skis, branches, or a climbing rope. When you combine some of the above with a sleeping bag, you have a carrier. Always tie the victim to it; this prevents further injury. Do not transport a person who may have suffered a possible back or neck fracture. Get help as fast as you can.

It is possible to carry someone for fairly long distances by using a strong branch as a "seat." The victim can sit on it, like on a garden swing. The person's arms should be at the level of the two rescuer's shoulders. Lightly injured people can be carried piggyback.

In cases where several people get hurt, leave one of your party with them. Another person can hasten to obtain help from the outside. Contact the nearest mountain rescue team, state or federal park or forest ranger, county sheriff's officer, the state highway patrol, or police officer. These are the authorities most concerned with rescue organization.

If you're near a highway, an ambulance may be summoned. Helicopters can sometimes land for extreme emergencies. But copters do not always operate safely in the West's high altitudes. The pilot needs visibility and cannot fly in strong winds.

It is important that the courier gives the rescuers all the necessary details. An effective message includes this data:

Time and place of accident
Nature of the injury
Name and condition of the victim
Terrain over which evacuation must take place
Special equipment or supplies necessary for rescue

Naturally, it is best to *prevent* mishaps in the first place.

Bibliography

Bridge, Raymond. *America's Backpacking Book*. New York: Charles Scribner's Sons, 1976.

Caldwell, John, *Cross-Country Skiing Today*. Brattleboro, VT: Stephen Greene Press.

Casewit, Curtis. *The Mountain World*. New York: Random House, 1976.

———. *The Mountaineering Handbook: An Invitation to Climbing*. Philadelphia: J. B. Lippincott, 1968.

———. *The Skiers' Handbook*. New York: Winchester Press, 1971.

Elman, Robert. *The Hiker's Bible*. New York: Doubleday, 1973.

Malo, John. *Snowmobiling: The Guide*. New York: Macmillan, 1971.

Mann, Bob. *Hot Dog Skiing*. New York: W. W. Norton, 1973.

Merrill, W. K. *The Hikers & Backpackers Handbook*. New York: Winchester Press, 1971.

Osgood, William, and Hurley, Leslie. *The Snowshoe Book*. Brattleboro, VT: Stephen Greene Press, 1975.

Perrin, A. T. *Explorers Sourcebook*. New York: Harper & Row.

Rebuffat, Gaston. *On Ice, Snow and Rock*. New York: Oxford University Press, 1971.

Index

ABOUT THE AUTHOR

Denver-based Curtis Casewit, a member of the Colorado Mountain Club and the U.S. Ski Writers, is the author of numerous books about the outdoors including *The Mountain World, Ski Fever, The Mountaineering Handbook,* and *The Skiers' Handbook.* He has traveled all over the world in search of material for *The Complete Book of Mountain Sports* and for his magazine articles.